UFO INVESTIGATION

BLITZ EDITIONS

Published by Blitz Editions
an imprint of Bookmart Ltd
Registered Number 2372865
Trading as Bookmart Ltd, Desford Road, Enderby
Leicester LE9 5AD

Cover design: Peter Dolton
Text design: Jim Reader
Production Manager: Sue Gray
Editorial Manager: Roz Williams

Printed in the Czech Republic
50973

ISBN 1 85605 128 5

Every effort has been made to contact the copyright holders for the pictures.
In some cases they have been untraceable, for which we offer our apologies.
Thanks to the Fortean Picture Library and the Hulton Deutsch Collection Ltd, who supplied most of them.
Pictures have been provided as follows: The Aetherius Society (pp 60, 65), M. De Cet (pp 5, 31 middle, 77, 78 top), Hulton Deutsch Collection Ltd (pp 4, 10 top, 11 right, 12 top, 19 middle, 20, 23, 42 top right, 43, 45, 46, 56, 61 bottom, 63, 68, 73, 75, 79 top), McDonnell Douglas Photos (31 bottom) and Orbis Publishing (31 top).
The remainder have been provided by the Fortean Picture Library.
Cover: Pictures have been supplied by the Fortean Picture Library.

The Author
Reuben Stone has long been fascinated by the paranormal and the mysteries of the unexplained. He is the author of many books and articles on military history, popular science and technology, and various aspects of anomalous phenomena.

UFO INVESTIGATION

HOW LONG HAVE THEY BEEN HERE?

On a bright summer's day an ordinary man witnessed an extraordinary sight. Kenneth Arnold's cautious reports unwittingly launched the age of the flying saucer. His was only one in a long series of inexplicable sightings.

At about 7 pm on the evening of 2 April 1991, Dick Feichtinger was driving to work in Faribault, Minnesota, when he saw a curious, white, long and narrow rectangular object apparently hanging in the sky above the town. 'It seemed to be hanging up and down. Rather than horizontal it was vertical,' he told reporter Paul Adams of the Faribault *Daily News*. 'The fact that it wasn't horizontal is strange...the configuration and the way it was hanging, that was what drew my attention to it.'

Still more remarkable was the fact that the object was there again when Feichtinger returned home from work later in the evening. Now, instead of being simply white, it was red and green. Once home, Feichtinger, naturally somewhat excited and more than intrigued, urged his wife and children to come and look at what he had seen. His family rushed to join him. As the Feichtingers watched, the object hanging mysteriously in the sky changed colour from red and green to solid white. By this time, neighbours had come out to see what the fuss was about, and were equally astonished to see the weird rectangle in the sky – which, they later agreed, 'seemed to be intelligently guided'.

At this point something very strange happened: two aircraft came cruising incredibly low over the houses. Said neighbour Steve Kelly: 'I thought they were going to land on my house.' And they were flying extremely slowly – so slowly that Dick Feichtinger commented:

Above: ***Kenneth Arnold, whose sighting of nine flying disks in the summer of 1947 ushered in the modern UFO era.***

Opposite: ***A 'daylight disk', photographed in October 1974 by David Knutsen in Surrey, British Columbia. The picture is typical of many of UFOs – devoid of detail, yet apparently showing a flying craft of unknown origin.***

Left: ***Kenneth Arnold collaborated with*** **Fate** ***magazine publisher Ray Palmer to tell the story of his sighting. Critics have alleged that Palmer sensationalized the book, but Arnold himself remained a sober and dedicated investigator.***

'I couldn't figure out what was keeping them up there.' Undaunted, he waved at them as he stood under a street light, and one of the planes seemed to acknowledge the wave by briefly turning on a set of floodlights – possibly its landing lights.

Before long, more aircraft were on the scene. Some witnesses said they counted up to 11 planes, including helicopters and two large aircraft. When the local military were contacted, however, they had no knowledge of any aircraft in the area besides a pair of National Air Guard C-130 Hercules cargo planes – one of which, spokesman Lt Kevin Gutknecht admitted, had indeed turned on its landing lights, although why was not explained. However, the C-130 pilots did not report seeing any strange lights in the vicinity of the town. A puzzled Lt Gutknecht was reported as saying: 'I have no idea what it is. It doesn't sound like anything we have in the Minnesota military inventory.'

THEY HAD NO DOUBT THAT THE WEIRD RECTANGLE IN THE SKY WAS GUIDED BY AN UNKNOWN INTELLIGENCE.

This case has all the ingredients of a certain kind of classic UFO sighting. There is the bizarre light in the sky, changing colour but seemingly under intelligent control, witnessed by a number of independent observers, none of whom apparently has any reason to lie, let alone organize a neighbourhood conspiracy. There are unexplained terrestrial aircraft associated with the sighting. The military deny all knowledge, as usual, although they give away a tantalizing and inexplicable detail: why did the Hercules pilot turn on his landing lights?

The role of the military in UFO lore is a subject on its own, but this case, like the hundreds of others reported each year, serves to illustrate that the UFO phenomenon is as strong as it ever was.

But how long have UFOs been seen in our skies?

Below: ***Harry S Truman, US President during the first sightings of 'flying saucers' after World War 2. Truman publicly stated his belief that UFOs were from outer space, and some ufologists believe that he instigated research into the phenomenon – research that remains super-secret even today.***

SUPER INTELLIGENCE

The modern history of UFOs is traditionally considered to begin in 1947, when Idaho businessman Kenneth Arnold saw nine weird disks of light flashing through the air while he was flying over the Cascade Mountains in Washington State, USA. This extraordinary encounter is worth recounting in detail, for it is a key episode in any attempt to understand what UFOs are – and what they have been. For Arnold's experience was by no means the first recorded instance of unexplained aerial objects and ordinary humanity coming into contact with each other. The great difference between his and previous sightings was the interpretation that was very soon put on it – that the lights Arnold saw were extra-terrestrial craft.

Hardly anyone in the Western world was immune to this belief. Even US President Harry S Truman could say, at a press conference on 4 April 1950, 'I can assure you that flying saucers...are not constructed by any power on Earth.' Just a few years later, in June 1954, at another conference in Innsbruck, Austria, Dr Herman Orberth – often called the 'father' of the German V-2 rocket, precursor of all the spacecraft launched from Earth – stated his conviction unmistakably: 'These objects are conceived and directed by intelligent beings of a very high order. They probably do not originate in our Solar System, perhaps not even in our galaxy.'

Whether or not UFOs are indeed material craft from outer space, messengers from alien civilizations, or the vehicles of galactic 'guardians' of humanity – or possibly even evidence of something far less benign that has a presence here on Earth – is a question that still vexes experts. The important point for the moment is that in the late 1940s, there was no other interpretation that made sense to most observers. Yet this was not Kenneth Arnold's own belief, and was certainly not the way that earlier witnesses saw the strange and bewildering lights and seemingly solid objects that from time to time have filled the skies throughout history and at the same time have filled the witnesses, too, with awe and wonder.

FLYING SAUCERS

Kenneth Arnold unwittingly launched the age of the flying saucer on the clear sunny afternoon of 24 June 1947. He was an experienced pilot, and that day was flying east across the Cascade Mountains from Chehalis to Yakima, Washington. Arnold had been enticed by the offer of a $5000 reward to spend an hour or so during his journey searching for a C-46 transport aircraft belonging to the US Marine Corps that had recently come down near Mount Rainier with 32 men on board. The Callair aircraft Arnold was flying was specially designed for working in the mountains. He took off from Chehalis airport at about 2 pm and made straight for the plateau of Mount Rainier.

Arnold was in the midst of his search at an altitude of about 9200 ft above the town of Mineral (about 25 miles south-west of the peak of Mount Rainier), and was making a 180° turn when 'a tremendously bright flash lit up the surfaces of my aircraft'. Understandably startled, Arnold thought at first that he was about to collide with another aircraft. He spent an anxious half-minute or so searching the sky for the source of the flash of light, but the only other plane in the vicinity was a Douglas DC-4 airliner, which he judged to be on the airlane from Seattle to San Francisco. Arnold then figured that he had seen the flash of the sun on the wings of a close-flying fighter; he thought he had been buzzed by a gung-ho young USAF lieutenant in a P-51, better known as the North American Aviation Mustang, the most powerful piston-engined fighter then in common service with the USAF.

Before he had time to start searching for a fast-moving Mustang, however, Arnold saw another flash – and this time saw where it came from. 'I observed,' he reported drily, 'far to my left and to the north, a formation of very bright objects coming from the vicinity of Mount Baker, flying very close to the mountain tops and travelling at tremendous speed.' Watching the craft near Mount Rainier, Arnold at first thought that he was watching a formation of nine jets at, he calculated, a distance of over 100 miles. 'What startled me most at this point was...that I could not find any tails on them.'

SCIENTISTS CONFIRMED THAT THE OBJECTS WERE CONTROLLED BY SUPER-INTELLIGENT BEINGS FROM ANOTHER GALAXY.

Above: ***A P-51 Mustang. When Kenneth Arnold first encountered mysterious flying disks in the air over the Cascade Mountains, his first thought was that he was being buzzed by one of these powerful fighters.***

The formation was flying almost directly across Arnold's own flightpath, which made it easy to make a rough calculation of the objects' speed, using the clock in his instrument panel, Mounts Rainier and Adams as markers, and reckoning the formation would pass about 23 miles in front of him. Arnold was amazed to discover that the nine craft were travelling at over 1700 mph – an astonishing speed for the time (it was only later that year that the sound barrier, about 750 mph, was first broken by a jet aircraft). What made this phenomenal speed all the more extraordinary was the way the craft were flying. Arnold said:

'They didn't fly like any aircraft I had

seen before...they flew in a definite formation, but erratically...their flight was like speed boats on rough water or similar to the tail of a Chinese kite that I once saw blowing in the wind...they fluttered and sailed, tipping their wings alternately and emitting those very bright blue-white flashes from their surfaces. At the time I did not get the impression that these flashes were emitted by them, but rather that it was the sun's reflection from the extremely highly polished surfaces of their wings.'

Above: ***George Adamski claimed to have photographed this 'mother ship' releasing smaller craft.***

Below: ***These UFOs have been dismissed by sceptics as a flight of geese.***

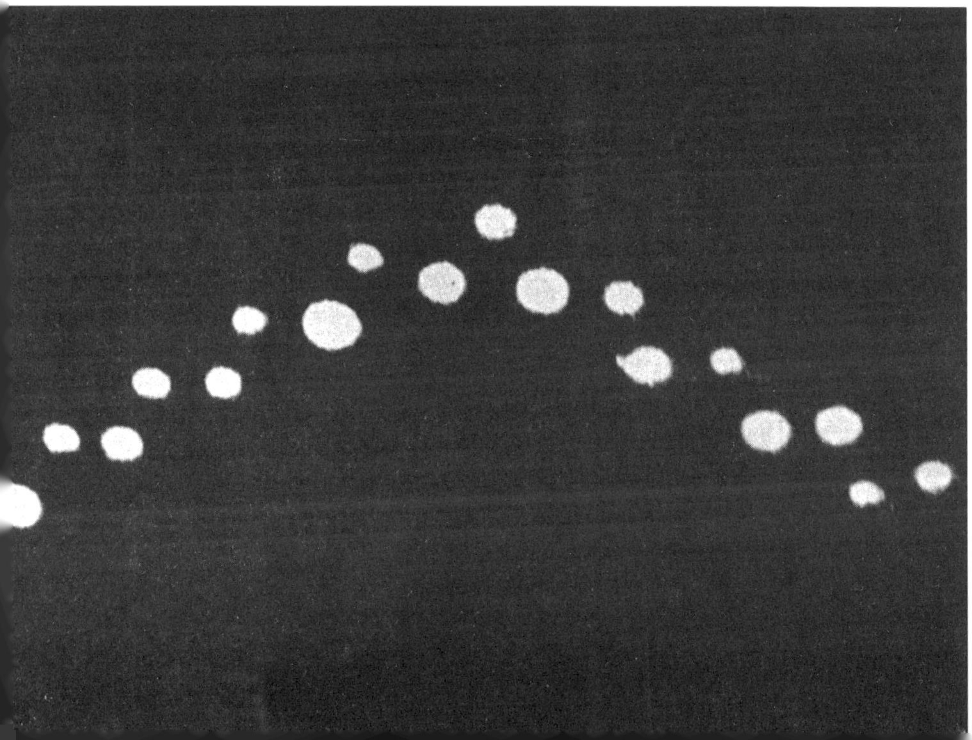

By the time the nine craft flew beyond the southernmost crest of Mount Adams, Arnold had decided to abandon his search for the missing C-46 and make for Yakima to report what he had seen. Landing there at about 4 pm, Arnold told his story to an airline manager and discussed it with other professional fliers, before taking off once more for Pendleton, Oregon. The news had travelled ahead of him: among the crowd of people to greet him there was Bill Becquette, from the local newspaper, the *East Oregonian*. It was during this time that Arnold described the craft he had seen as flying 'like a saucer would if you skipped it across the water'. This description was slightly garbled by Becquette, who thus originated the phrase 'flying saucers'. Then, with other pilots, Arnold cautiously recalculated his estimate of the UFOs' extraordinary speed. But even the most conservative reckoning still put their velocity at over 1350 mph. From talking to other airmen, Arnold was now convinced that he had seen a flight of guided missiles, 'robotly controlled'. He concluded that the government had chosen this way to announce the discovery of 'a new principle of flight'.

Then the story broke, put out on the Associated Press wire by Bill Becquette. For three days at Pendleton Arnold was besieged with enquiries. Finally, exhausted and unable to work, Arnold flew the 200 miles across the state line to his home in Boise, Indiana. It was shortly after arriving there that Arnold had a telephone call from Dave Johnson, aviation editor of the *Idaho Statesman*. That conversation changed everything for Arnold. As he put it:

'The doubt he displayed of the authenticity of my story told me, and I am sure he was in a position to know, that it was not a new military guided missile and that if what I had seen was true it did not belong to the good old USA. It was then that I really began to wonder.'

ALIEN CRAFT

Arnold might well have wondered, for in the three days that he was being harassed by newshounds he discovered that his was by no means the only, or even the first, sighting of such mysterious flying objects. ('I thought it wouldn't be long before there was one of these things in every garage,' he commented wryly, at the stage when he still believed that he had seen a flight of government-sponsored machines.)

In April 1947, a meteorologist tracking a weather balloon saw a saucer-shaped object fly by – a neat irony, as so many later UFO sightings have been explained away as, and sometimes have really been, misidentifications of weather balloons. On 5 May, a 'silvery object' was reported to have dropped out of the sky over Washington State and disintegrated before reaching the ground. On 12 June, shortly before Arnold's own experience, another chain of UFOs was seen over Weiser, Idaho, and on 14 June a pilot named Rankin also observed a flight of 10 saucer-like objects flying in triangular formation. At about the same time as Arnold saw 'his' flying disks, a prospector in the Cascades also witnessed a similar group of UFOs, whose presence made his compass needle go wild. Arnold's sighting in fact took place in the midst of a major UFO 'flap' – a flurry of sightings – in the late spring and summer of 1947. Between the beginning of June and 16 July that year, the US authorities received over 850 reports of UFOs from all over the USA. By September, the USAF had set up Project Sign to evaluate the reports and, among other things, consider the possibility that these were extra-terrestrial craft.

What made Arnold's report different was that it sparked an equally monumental flap in the media – whose underlying assumption throughout was that 'flying saucers' were indeed alien craft, and were probably not very friendly.

Curiously enough, Arnold himself did not share this view of the origins of UFOs. In 1962, in the magazine *Flying Saucers*, he published his own conclusion: '...the so-called unidentified flying objects that have been seen in our atmosphere are not space ships from another planet at all, but are groups and masses of living organisms that are as much a part of our atmosphere and space as the life we find in the depths of our oceans. The only major difference [is] that they have a natural ability to change their densities at will.'

Arnold, perhaps, was not a man of his age; but this was not the first time that UFOs had been identified with living things in the sky. On the other hand, the belief that they were nuts-and-bolts machines was not entirely new, either.

MACHINES OF DEATH

Probably the earliest report of a UFO on record is to be found in (of all places) a treatment of architecture and civic planning called the *Samarangana-Sartradhara*, an ancient Indian text that dates back at least to 500 BC. In this, one passage describes curious machines called *vimanas*, which can fly, and are controlled by pilots. There follows a number of lengthy descriptions of how the *vimanas*' various power systems work, but they are tantalizingly obscure. The same devices are also mentioned in the great Hindu epics in Sanskrit, the *Mahabharata* and *Ramayana*, where they are described as military machines with the range to 'carry death' anywhere in the world – an assertion that, like so many aspects of unexplained and paranormal phenomena, raises as many questions as it

SHAKEN BY HIS EXPERIENCE, ARNOLD WAS CONVINCED THAT HE HAD SEEN A FLIGHT OF ROBOT-GUIDED MISSILES.

GREAT HINDU EPICS DESCRIBED THE 'MACHINES OF DEATH' IN CHILLING DETAIL – WERE THE WRITERS FORETELLING A CATASTROPHIC NUCLEAR WAR?

Above: ***Shooting stars – seen here in a Victorian print – were taken to be portents in more superstitious times. Today, misinterpretations of such natural phenomena tend to have a technological flavour, and many reported 'UFOs' are in fact meteorites.***

Below: ***In medieval times and before, mysterious aerial phenomena were often believed to be dragons. But did people actually see dragons then, just as witnesses report seeing flying disks today? If so, have UFOs changed in appearance over the centuries to suit expectations?***

answers. One researcher has even gone so far as to say that 'we cannot but be struck [when reading these works] by the modernity of certain passages, where we seem to be reading an account of a nuclear war'.

Roman writers noted visitations by UFOs: Livy (59 BC–AD 17) described a sighting in 214 BC at Hadria in Italy that looked like an altar in the sky, while Pliny the Elder (AD 23–79) refers to 'gleaming beams in the sky' in his *De Rerum Naturae*, and describes how in 66 BC a 'spark' fell from a star to the Earth, became as large as the Moon, and then – shrinking in size – returned to the sky. And in his *Historia Naturalis*, Pliny makes an intriguing assertion:

'A light from the sky by night, the phenomenon usually called "night suns" was seen in the consulship of Gaius Caecilius and Gnaeus Papirius and often on other occasions causing apparent daylight in the night. In the consulship of Lucius Valerius and Gaius Marius a burning shield scattering sparks ran across the sky at sunset from east to west.'

The fascinating part of this passage is the words 'usually called'. Pliny seems to assume that 'night suns' were, if not commonplace, at least well-enough known to have a common name. And, although he was one of the first naturalists, Pliny was enough a man of his time to accept such wonders without comment.

The literature of medieval Europe abounds in UFO reports of various kinds. Among the earliest are to be found in the works of St Gregory, bishop of Tours in France in the 6th century. In his *Historia Francorum* ('History of the Franks'), the saint related how in AD 584 'there appeared in the sky brilliant rays of light which seemed to cross and collide with one another', while the following year 'in the month of September, certain people saw signs, that is to say rays or domes such as are customarily seen...to race across the sky'. Elsewhere he describes 'golden globes' that, on several occasions, flashed at speed across the skies of France. St Gregory also wrote seven volumes concerning miracles and – in keeping with his devout Christianity – seems to have been in little doubt that these were heavenly signs. The interpretation, in short, fitted the preconceptions of the chronicler.

In the same way, in AD 793, the *Anglo-Saxon Chronicle* reported: 'In this year terrible portents appeared in Northumbria, and miserably afflicted the inhabitants; these were exceptional flashes of lightning, and fiery dragons were seen flying through the air.' The *Chronicle* was written by secular scribes, and their report reflects the still thickly pagan atmosphere of 8th-

century England – for both people and place were far less orthodox in their Christianity than the monasteries of France had been two centuries previously. What today would have been called a UFO or even a 'flying saucer' was to them a dragon. It flew in the air, it lit up the sky, and it was fearsome and inherently inexplicable; it was a dragon because that was the nearest thing in human knowledge to match what people actually saw. This unconscious mental process also helps to explain why diehard sceptics, confronted with a UFO, will always believe they have seen the planet Venus, or a weather balloon – indeed anything other than an inexplicable and possibly alien craft.

Just as people see UFOs today, people saw dragons then. Kenneth Arnold was not the first to suggest that UFOs, in the most literal sense of being unidentified flying objects, were members of the animal kingdom. In England in 1113, a group of churchmen from Laon in France were going from town to town in Wessex (south-west England), bearing with them relics of the Virgin Mary, which they used to perform miracles of healing. At the coastal town of Christchurch, Hampshire, they were astonished to see a dragon come up out of the sea, 'breathing fire out of its nostrils'. There are plenty of reports of modern UFOs rising out of the sea, as well.

The 12th-century chronicler Ralph Niger recounts that on 9 March 1170, at St Osyth in Essex, south-east England, 'a wonderfully large dragon was seen, borne up from the Earth through the air. The air was kindled into fire by its motion and burnt a house, reducing it and its outbuildings to ashes.'

Dragons and UFOs show some interesting parallels. Whatever form UFOs take, they are always perceived as being on the very edge of human knowledge as it exists in any particular era, including some alluring extras that we can imagine but cannot (yet) achieve – such as faster-than-light travel today, or heavier-than-air flight in the Middle Ages.

Like UFOs today, dragons were familiar as *ideas*, but were also regarded as

Above: ***An astonishing aerial battle breaks out over the city of Nuremberg on 4 April 1561. A contemporary account speaks of a 'very frightful spectacle', in which luminous globes, crosses and tubes appeared to fight one another for about an hour in broad daylight. All then fell to earth, 'as if on fire'. The citizens saw this bizarre display as a divine warning to improve their sinful ways – but ufologists are divided over whether the event had its origins in a highly unusual freak of nature or some more alien source.***

Right: ***Edmund Halley was a pioneer of the scientific observation of astronomical events, and also seriously investigated reports of anomalous and enigmatic phenomena – in striking contrast to the attitude of much of today's scientific establishment.***

Below: ***A huge meteorite falls to Earth. Many apparent UFO reports from before the 20th century may refer to natural events like this, but just as many accounts describe extraordinary and inexplicable behaviour on the part of the heavenly lights.***

'impossible' in practical terms. To the medieval mind, dragons occupied a strange no-man's land between reality and imagination. Most people had not seen one – though they might know someone who had, or who knew someone else who had. But everyone was familiar with dragons and what they did (which was guard treasure, breathe fire, and fly), and everyone knew what a dragon looked like. Medieval people would have had no difficulty in identifying one if it landed in a bustling market place and snorted smoke and flame. But actual dragons remained elusive and magical, neither quite real nor quite imaginary, possible but improbable. Today, most of the same things could be said about UFOs, except that they are only magical in the sense that they are 'otherworldly' or paranormal.

AERIAL CONFLICT

As time went on, and the old Anglo-Saxon myths disappeared from memory in an England conquered by the Normans, the identification of UFOs with dragons faded too. The persistent appearance of inexplicable lights and objects in the sky did not fade with them, however. In his *Historia Anglorum* ('The History of the English'), another English chronicler, Matthew of Paris, tells how at sunset on 24 July 1239, 'a great star like a torch appeared. It rose in the south and climbed the sky giving out a great light...it left behind it smoke and sparks. It was shaped like a great head, the front part was sparkling and the back part gave out smoke and flashes.' And in his memoirs the French Duke of Bourgogne recalled that on 1 November 1461, an object appeared in the sky 'as long and wide as a half-moon; it hung stationary for about a quarter hour, clearly visible, then suddenly...spiralled, twisted and turned like a spring and rose into the heavens'.

Such accounts were not limited to Europe: records of strange lights over Japan go back at least to the 10th century, while in May 1606 the former capital of Japan, Kyoto, saw a succession of fireballs in the sky. One of them hovered near the Nijo castle in front of a host of witnesses, spinning like a red wheel.

And so the records continue: blue, black and blood-red balls, along with disks and blood-red crosses and two huge cylinders, battled together in the skies over Nuremberg, Germany, on 4 April 1561, and there was a similar aerial conflict a little more than five years later over Basel,

Switzerland, between black spheres: 'many became red and fiery, ending by being consumed and vanishing', wrote the 'student in sacred writings and the liberal arts', one Samuel Coccius, who reported the weird events of 7 August 1566 in the city's gazette.

A SKY OF FLAMES

In the centuries that followed, observers, including the astronomer Edmund Halley (1656–1742), continued to note a host of bizarre aerial phenomena. But now the tone of the reports starts to change yet again: as the so-called 'Age of Reason' dawned in the late 17th century and rigorously 'logical' scientific observation became the order of the day, so different explanations for sightings of what we would now call UFOs begin to creep in to the accounts. At Sheffield, England, on 9 December 1731, for instance, at about 5 pm, Thomas Short saw what he later described as 'a dark red cloud, below which was a luminous body which emitted intense beams of light…the light beams moved slowly for a while, then stopped. Suddenly it became so hot that I could take off my shirt even though I was out of doors [this in the dead of winter!]. This meteor was observed over Kilkenny, Ireland, where it seemed like a great ball of fire. It was reported that it shook the entire island and that the whole sky seemed to burst into flames.'

In the afternoon of the next day, local manuscript records show, this 'meteor' appeared over Romania: '…there appeared in the west a great sign in the sky, blood-red and very large. It stayed in place for two hours, then separated into two parts which then rejoined, and the object disappeared towards the west.' To the Romanian mind of the time, this was 'a sign'; to the cultured gentleman of Augustan England, it was a 'meteor', if a very strange one by our modern standards of judging meteors. The tendency to interpret such events according to the most easily available *existing* explanation – and one that at the time was the most acceptable socially – is even clearer in another account from 18th-century England.

On 18 August 1783, a small crowd of the gentry that included Dr James Lind (whose pioneering dietary work resulted in the eradication of scurvy from the Royal Navy), the renowned water-colour painter Thomas Sandby and the scientist Tiberius Cavallo, were on the terrace at the royal

In August 1783, a group of distinguished writers, artists and scientists that included medical pioneer Dr James Lind **(above)** ***witnessed the appearance of a weird luminous cloud, which seemed to be under intelligent control, over Windsor Castle*** **(left).**

residence of Windsor Castle enjoying the summer evening when, according to Cavallo's account published the next year by the Royal Society, at about 9.45 pm they 'suddenly saw appear an oblong cloud moving more or less parallel to the horizon. Under this cloud could be seen a luminous object which soon became spherical, brilliantly lit, which came to a halt...This strange sphere seemed at first to be pale blue in colour, but its luminosity increased and soon it set off again towards the east. Then the object changed direction and moved parallel to the horizon before disappearing to the south-east...the light it gave out was prodigious; it lit up everything on the ground. Before it vanished it changed its shape, became oblong, and at the same time as a sort of trail appeared, it seemed to separate into two small bodies. Scarcely two minutes later the sound of an explosion was heard.'

To the scientist Cavallo, the group had

The mysterious airships that plagued parts of the United States in 1896 and 1897 (right: *a contemporary illustration from the* Chicago Times-Herald) *were far in advance of American airship technology of the day and, according to all reports, far bigger than anything that did eventually fly – as can be seen from the scale of this early Spencer airship* (above), *taking off at Ranelagh in 1903.*

clearly witnessed a meteor: the proof was in the explosion, presumably made as the thing crashed to earth. The astonishing thing to modern eyes is the similarity between the cloud and the object beneath it seen in 1783, and the almost identical nature of the other so-called 'meteor' that visited England, Ireland and Romania some half a century before. But a person trained to look out for meteors will see them when something like one appears in the sky, however remotely like an actual meteor it may seem from our later perspective.

THE ALIENS HAVE LANDED

True to form, the next century saw another, no less consistent, interpretation of unexplained aerial phenomena. The Victorian era saw an astonishing leap forward in works of engineering, especially in transport – from the spread of railways around the globe to the introduction of iron steamships capable of crossing the Atlantic, and the production of the first cars. Land and sea had been conquered: but not the air. Airships seemed the most promising means of achieving sustained, controlled flight, but the major problem was power. It was not until light, compact internal combustion engines appeared in the late 1890s that airships became truly practicable. By then, they were being discussed everywhere – both as the next great advance in engineering, and as something more strange.

On 6 November 1896, the citizens of Sacramento, California, were amazed to see a light moving sedately through the night sky, apparently carried by a cigar-shaped craft. During the month further reports of this machine poured in from all over California. From March 1897, the American Great Lakes states and Texas were plagued by reports of lights in the sky, some like 'electric arc lights', others shaped like balls or wheels, that were attached to huge craft – which was at once dubbed an airship – shaped like a cigar, an egg, or a barrel, and apparently powered by propellers. On a number of occasions these machines landed, and the occupants, who appeared to be ordinary human beings, spoke to bemused witnesses on the ground.

Below: ***Ludvig Lindbäck points to where his brother Knut saw a mysterious rocket crash into Lake Kölmjärv, Sweden, on 19 July 1946. The Swedish government received some 1000 such reports in 1946, but the country's top aviation and rocketry experts were unable to provide an explanation – and none has been forthcoming since.***

Right: ***Karl-Gösta Bartoll trawls the bottom of Lake Kölmjärv in a fruitless attempt to find wreckage from the 'rocket' that crashed there in July 1946.***

The case for the alien origin of UFOs rests on numerous eyewitness reports – and many tantalizing photographs, whose credibility is usually in inverse proportion to their quality. James Lucci was taking a time exposure of the Moon over Beaver, Pennsylvania, on 8 August 1965, when, he claimed, this UFO* (opposite above) *came into view. Many ufologists have concluded not only that UFOs are alien, but that the US government has retrieved crashed saucers like this one* (artist's impression, opposite below), *which allegedly was taken to Fort Riley, Kansas, in November 1964.

Then, at the beginning of May 1897, the reports dried up.

An airship as large as the objects that witnesses described would have had to be rigid, or it would have been uncontrollable. But it was not until 1900 that the development of rigid airships – 'dirigibles' – began, and that was in Germany. No airship then flying, either in the USA or elsewhere, was capable of the feats performed by these machines – if that is what they were. The first dirigible to fly in the USA was Thomas Baldwin's *California Arrow*, which took off from Oakland, near San Francisco, California, in 1904.

In August 1946, the Swedish authorities received nearly 1000 reports of mysterious rockets in their skies, some of which crashed spectacularly into the country's inland lakes. One theory was that the Soviets were testing captured German V-2 rockets – which, in the public eye at least, were the most advanced technology of the day. But Swedish aviation engineers, who by then had considerable knowledge of the V-2, failed to find any plausible explanation. Similar displays of rocket-like behaviour by mysterious aerial objects were reported early the following month by British Army units in Greece, especially around Thessaloniki. Midway through September they were seen in Portugal, and then in Belgium.

IS OURS THE AGE WHEN THE WATCHERS IN OUTER SPACE WILL REVEAL THEIR TRUE PURPOSE TO US? ARE THEY OUR FRIENDS, OUR GUARDIANS – OR OUR MASTERS?

THE WATCHERS IN OUTER SPACE

UFOs have been seen in the form of dragons, meteors, airships, rockets...and as 'flying saucers'. To the sceptic, all these bizarre sightings are either natural phenomena, errors of perception or plain hallucination. Some, perhaps most, UFO sightings certainly are no more than that. There is certainly good evidence that many truly strange lights in the sky are the product of little-known and rarely seen natural forces, which seem to be released in areas of geological disturbance – along fault lines in the Earth's crust, for example. Such a theory may well explain a proportion, at least, of the long history of mysterious airborne lights over Japan, which is notoriously prone to earthquakes. But these explanations don't account for the UFO phenomenon as a whole.

The common belief since Kenneth Arnold's sighting in 1947 has been that UFOs are extra-terrestrial craft built by a civilization that is technologically far in advance of our own. There are very strong grounds for questioning this assumption, but it remains a possibility. Some of the people who claim to have spoken to aliens and extra-terrestrials also maintain that this civilization has been watching the Earth for a very long time. Presumably, there have been occasions when – for reasons we can only guess at – they have been unable to conceal their presence entirely. Or perhaps they have deliberately shown themselves, as part of a centuries-long programme of gently introducing themselves to us. In either case, when they have been obliged or have chosen to reveal themselves, they have come in clever disguises: just far enough within the bounds of human understanding, carefully matching the mood of the times, to be acceptable, if strange – and just far enough beyond normality to deter unwanted investigation or interference.

And we may just be living in the age when they have decided to reveal their true purposes to us.

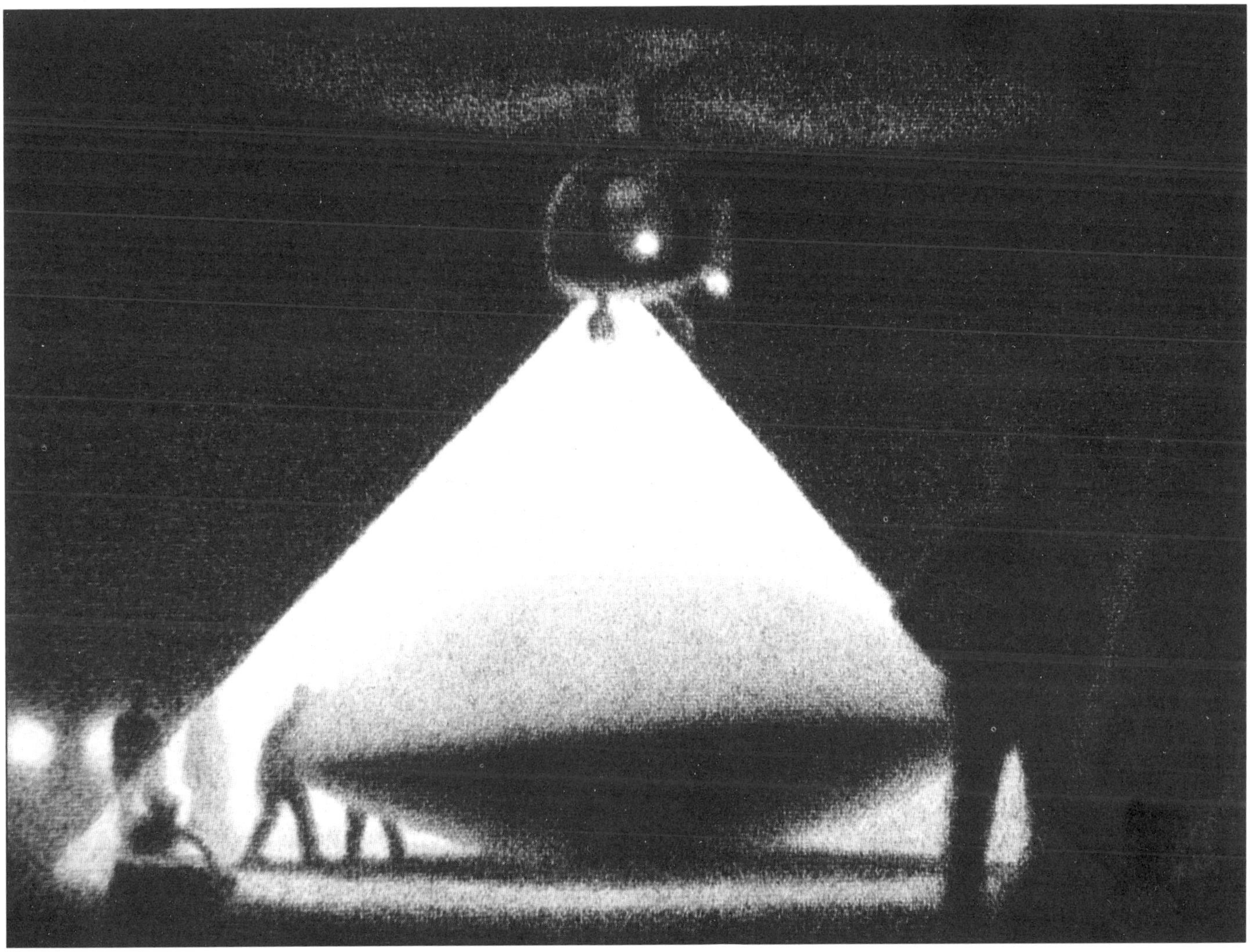

MESSENGERS FROM OUTER SPACE

George Adamski had spent years observing the skies on the lookout for UFOs. An impulse drew him into the desert where a figure beckoned him from the opening of a ravine...but with a sudden chill of fear he wondered whether his long vigil had been wise.

Is someone – or something – inhabiting the Solar System besides ourselves? Are they out there watching us, for some mysterious purpose of their own, or are they simply our elusive neighbours? Are they friendly or are they hostile?

The answers to these questions – the most perplexing and, many would say, the most crucial in the whole debate about UFOs – should have become apparent in the decades since UFOs first revealed themselves as inexplicable flying disks. For in that time numerous people have claimed to have had direct contact with the occupants of UFOs. One might expect a clear picture to emerge from these undoubtedly traumatic experiences of who the aliens are, where they are from, and what – if anything – they want. Yet cases of contactees, and more especially those of people who have been abducted by UFOs, present some of the most conflicting and perplexing evidence of all the vast array of data in the field of ufology.

There are, essentially, three kinds of witness who might help answer some of the fundamental questions.

First, there are those people who have come so close to UFOs that they have seen and described the occupants.

Second, there are those who have been approached by aliens in a friendly spirit and have come away with what amounts to 'a message for mankind' – not necessarily of enormous cosmic import, but at least containing some explanation of what the aliens are doing and why they are here.

Third, there is a small group of people who seem to have been forcibly abducted by aliens. These cases are the most difficult to assess and contain the most astounding claims: that the contactees were subjected to some kind of medical examination, for example, and in some cases were sexually used or abused.

EVADING CAPTURE

One of the most frustrating aspects of the UFO enigma is the inconsistency of the evidence. This is particularly apparent in the descriptions of alien beings given by those who claim to have seen them.

The first such contactee to come to public attention was George Adamski, a part-time caterer who described himself as a 'philosopher and teacher' and who lived in Palomar Gardens, on the southern slopes of Mount Palomar, California. Adamski's passion was astronomy; he had a 15 in and a 6in reflector telescope set up at home to watch the stars. He was also convinced that the other planets of our Solar System were inhabited. On 9 October 1946, while watching a meteor shower from his home, he saw what he later believed to be confirmation of his conviction. Along with others he saw 'a gigantic space craft' that was 'hovering high above the mountain ridge to the south of Mount Palomar, toward San Diego'. It was 'a large black object, resembling a gigantic dirigible'.

Above: ***George Adamski's remarkable adventures with purported visitors from Venus were first chronicled in*** **Flying Saucers Have Landed.** ***Desmond Leslie's part of the book described many historical accounts of apparent UFO sightings.***

Opposite: ***Adamski, who before his contact with alleged Venusians was a keen amateur astronomer, with one of his telescopes.***

Below: ***Adamski, with Long John Nebel and the 'mother ship' and attendant saucers that he claimed to have photographed in March 1951.***

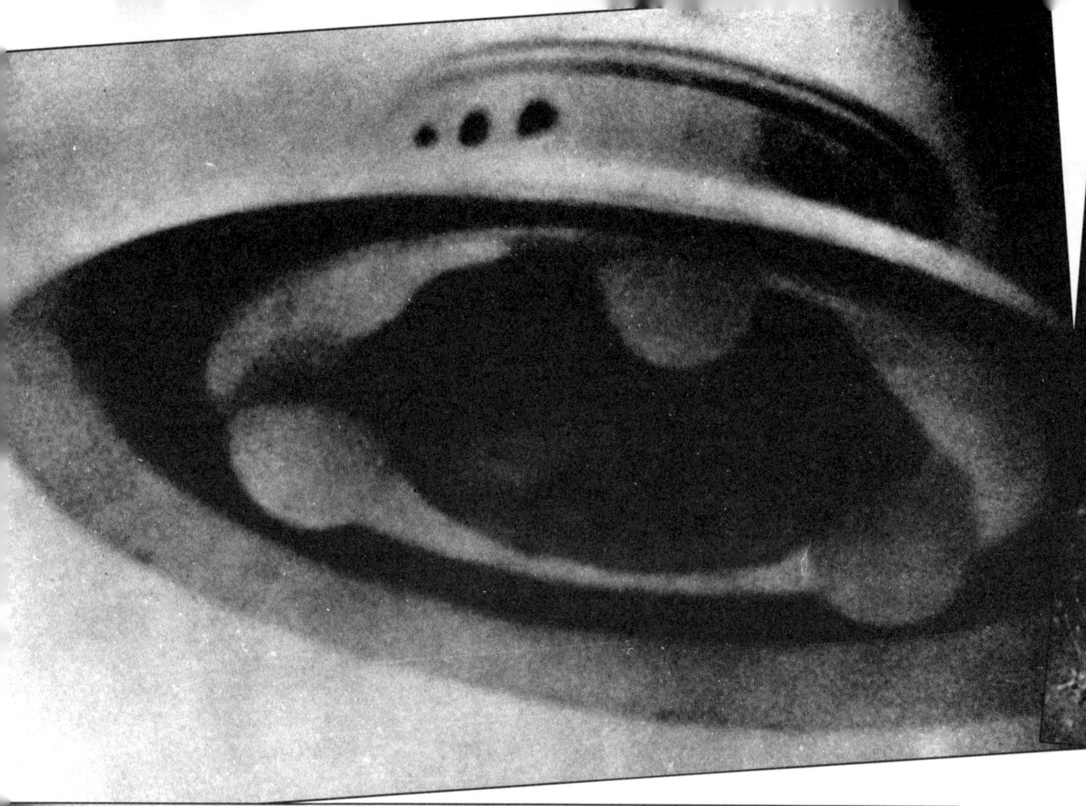

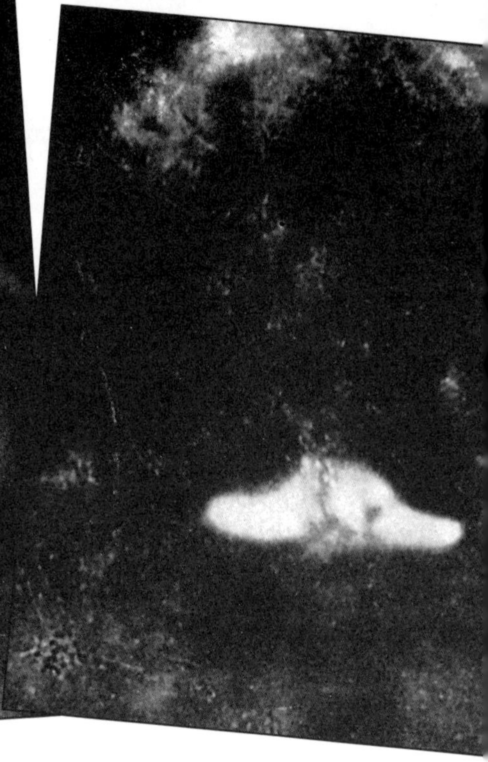

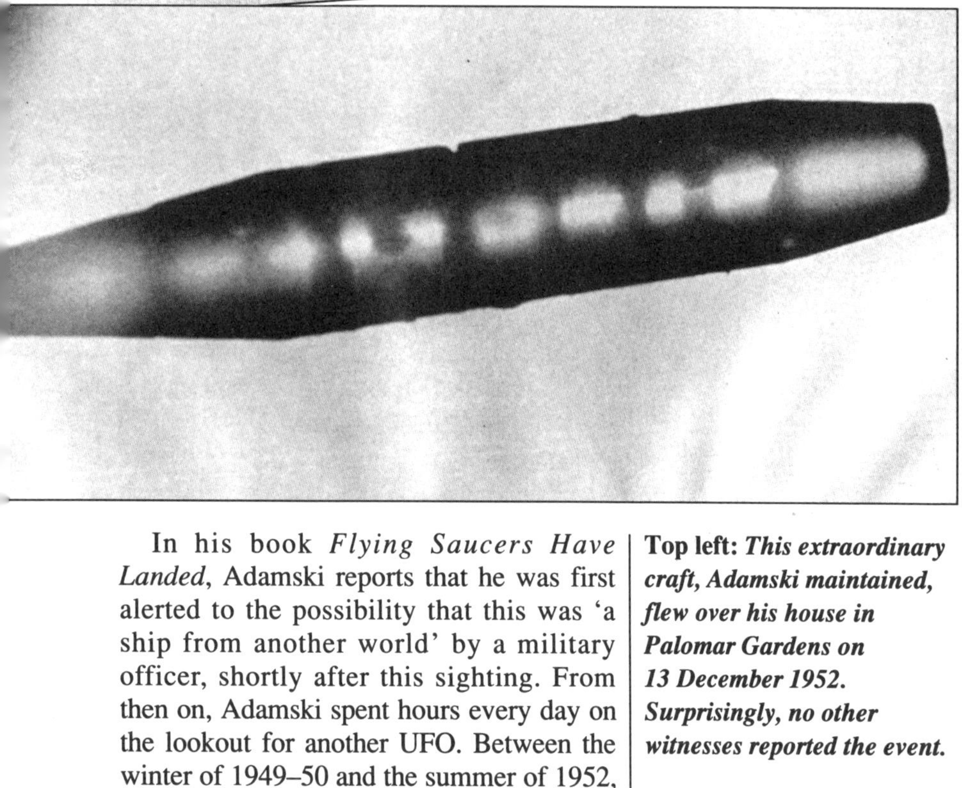

In his book *Flying Saucers Have Landed*, Adamski reports that he was first alerted to the possibility that this was 'a ship from another world' by a military officer, shortly after this sighting. From then on, Adamski spent hours every day on the lookout for another UFO. Between the winter of 1949–50 and the summer of 1952, he photographed a number of UFOs both with and without his 6 in telescope, some 18 of the photos being of high quality. Adamski began giving lectures on UFOs and extra-terrestrials to various interested groups, and as a result of these contacts began to hear rumours that flying saucers had been landing in 'various desert areas not a great drive from Mount Palomar'.

On 20 November 1952, Adamski, his secretary Mrs Lucy McKinnis, and the proprietor of Palomar Gardens, Mrs Alice K. Wells, met up with four such contacts – Mr and Mrs Al C. Bailey of Winslow, Arizona, and Dr and Mrs George H. Williamson of Prescott, Arizona – on the highway near Blythe, California, to go into the desert in the hope of seeing a UFO land. Adamski gives no reason for having chosen this day rather than another, but admits to following a hunch as to where they should start their vigil – about 11 miles down the highway from Desert Center toward Parker, Arizona. The group was richly rewarded.

After a stroll and a light lunch, the party sat scanning the sky. The only thing of note was the passage of a two-engine plane apparently on a routine flight. Then:

'Suddenly and simultaneously we all turned as one [*sic*] looking again toward the closest mountain ridge where just a few minutes before the first plane had crossed. Riding high, and without sound, there was a gigantic cigar-shaped silvery ship, without wings or appendages of any kind.'

The craft moved as if drifting in the direction of the group, then stopped, hovering. Adamski felt that the ship had come specifically for him, and on another hunch demanded to be taken down the road – the spot they were in, next to a well-travelled highway, was too conspicuous, he thought, and would discourage a landing.

With Lucy McKinnis at the wheel and Al Bailey accompanying, Adamski was driven off the highway onto a dirt road, while all the time the giant ship followed them silently. After half a mile or so they stopped. Here, Adamski set up his smaller

Top left: ***This extraordinary craft, Adamski maintained, flew over his house in Palomar Gardens on 13 December 1952. Surprisingly, no other witnesses reported the event.***

Top right: ***This picture, according to Adamski, shows a UFO traversing the disk of the Moon on 6 June 1950.***

Above: ***This cigar-shaped UFO was photographed by Adamski on 1 May 1952. Unfortunately, there are no background or other contextual details by which the size or true nature of the image can be judged.***

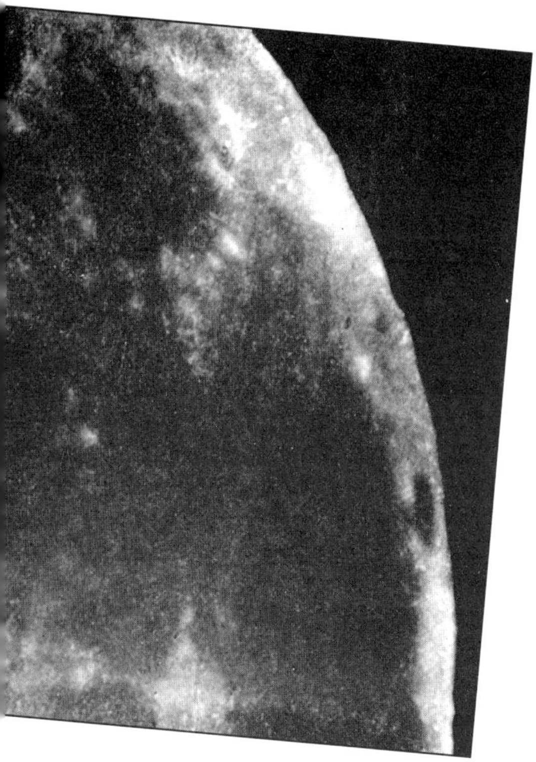

telescope and a camera and then, fearing the presence of his companions would deter the aliens, sent them back to their original parking spot, to watch from there. As they left, a number of aircraft – presumably fighters – roared into sight and tried to circle the huge craft above. In response, the ship 'turned its nose upward and shot out into space'. Wondering if the planes had chased it away for good, Adamski settled down to wait.

Before five minutes was up, he saw a flash in the sky and 'almost instantly a beautiful craft appeared to be drifting through a saddle between two of the mountain peaks'. It settled on a ridge, and Adamski took photographs. Then it lifted and flew back across the saddle, as two more aircraft came into sight, circled, and flew on. Apparently the saucer had evaded them. After some minutes Adamski realized that a man was beckoning him from the opening of a ravine about 450 yds away. Wondering who this was, Adamski made his way toward the figure. Only when he was within arm's length of the man did Adamski realize that he was looking at a visitor from another world.

A WARNING

'The beauty of his form surpassed anything I had ever seen,' he wrote later. That form was unmistakably human. The man was about 5 ft 6 in tall, weighed about 135 lb, and appeared – in Earthly terms – to be about 28 years old. He had shoulder-length, sandy-coloured wavy hair 'glistening more beautifully than any woman's I have ever seen'. His skin was the colour of a suntanned Caucasian's. His face was round, and he had an extremely high forehead, 'calm, grey-green eyes' that slanted slightly at the corners, high cheekbones, and a 'finely chiselled' nose. He seemed to be beardless. The alien was wearing a single-piece, finely woven chocolate-brown suit with no visible fasteners or pockets, but with a broad waistband and a close-fitting high collar. His shoes were ox-blood red and had blunt toes. Adamski thought the outfit was a uniform of some kind.

His attempts to speak to the creature failed, but by concentrating his efforts Adamski succeeded in communicating with a mixture of hand signals and telepathy.

A NUMBER OF SMALL FIGHTER PLANES TRIED VAINLY TO ENCIRCLE THE GARGANTUAN SPACECRAFT.

Below: ***The first photograph of Venus's full disk taken by a spacecraft from Earth – the NASA Pioneer Orbiter, in 1979. The planet's turbulent atmosphere – incapable of supporting humanoid life, despite Adamski's claims to have met a native – is clearly visible.***

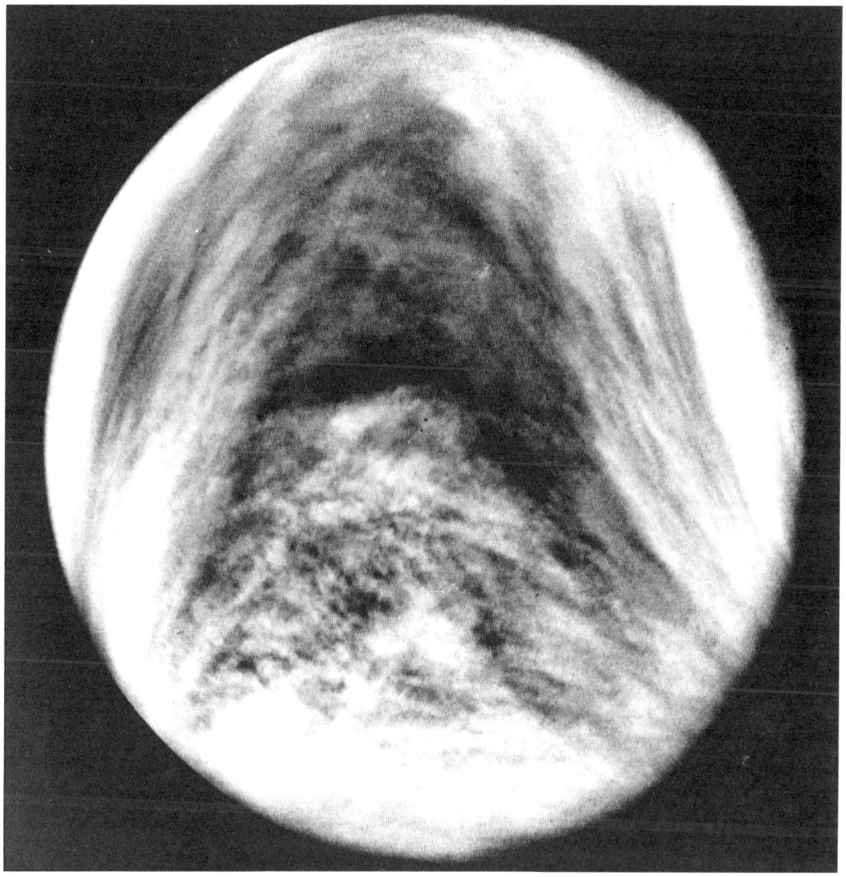

The first thing the alien told Adamski in this manner was that he was from the planet Venus. The Venusians were here, he said, because they were concerned about radiation from atomic explosions: too many of these explosions would destroy all of Earth.

THE WARNING WAS SIMPLE – THE EARTH WAS GOING TO BE DESTROYED.

Below: ***'A giant leap for mankind' – one of the Apollo 11 crew on the Moon. As human knowledge of the Solar System became more accurate and detailed, so visiting UFO occupants stopped claiming to have come from neighbouring planets and made more and more extravagant claims. Some ufologists maintain that this is part of a game that aliens are playing with humanity – and some are certain that the game is a disguise for the fact that the aliens are not from outer space at all.***

And so it went on. The saucer which brought the Venusian – who did not divulge his name – to Earth had been launched from within the atmosphere by the giant 'mother ship' that Adamski had seen earlier. The craft was powered by 'magnetism'. Asked if he believed in God, the spaceman replied yes, but observed that Venusians lived according to the laws of the Creator and not the laws of materialism as Earthmen did. People from the other planets in the Solar System – all of which were inhabited – and from other systems too were visiting Earth. Some of their craft had crashed on Earth, shot down by 'men of this world'. Saucers landed only in remote places to avoid panicking people, but the time would come when they would land near centres of population. There were many aliens living in our midst already, and for this reason the Venusian refused to be photographed, lest his features become recognizable. All aliens were essentially human in form.

Adamski was then allowed to approach the saucer hovering nearby, but was not permitted inside it. After this, the Venusian climbed aboard his craft, and it glided silently away.

DESOLATE OF LIFE

It is interesting, to say the least, that as Earth's own space programme developed during the 1960s, and probes reported with monotonous regularity that our neighbouring planets were incapable of supporting life as we know it, so the occupants of UFOs have stopped claiming to come from our Solar System. They would certainly feel uncomfortable on Venus, which has an atmospheric pressure 94.5 times higher than our own – which alone would cause any Venusian lacking massive pressurized body armour to explode the moment he set foot on Earth – while temperatures are commonly around 900°F (five times hotter than the boiling point of water). Venusian rain consists largely of hydrochloric and sulphuric acid, and the 'air' is almost entirely carbon dioxide.

However, bearing in mind that one of the few consistent aspects of the UFO phenomenon is its habit of staying just within the borders of the human imagination, it makes some sense for an alien to suggest that he comes from a place that the apparently rather backward terrestrials can immediately recognize as habitable. And in 1952 many people did believe that Venus could support life. Even then, they were wrong – for as early as the 1920s scientists had deduced that Venus could either support 'only low forms of life...mostly belonging to the vegetable kingdom' or was a desert planet plagued by dust storms. By 1932 the Venusian atmosphere was known to be mainly carbon dioxide. This meant that even vegetation was absent.

By 1975, hardly anyone in the Western world was ill-informed about space: six years earlier, the first attempt to put men on the Moon had succeeded brilliantly, while a host of unmanned craft had been sent out to explore remote space, sending back extraordinary pictures of the Solar System along with a mass of information about its planetary environments. All were clearly desolate of any known forms of life.

AN INSANE SOCIETY

Just after 2 pm on 28 January 1975, a one-armed farmer named Eduard 'Billy' Meier was walking near his home at Hinwel, in the canton of Zürich in Switzerland, when he saw a silvery, disk-shaped craft swoop down with a strange throbbing sound out of the sky and land about 100 yds away from him. Intrigued, he began to run toward it, but some invisible force halted him after about 50 yds. A figure then emerged from the disk, which was about 25 ft in diameter, and approached him. When it and its vehicle departed an hour and 45 minutes later, Billy Meier knew he had met a cosmonaut from the Pleiades star cluster (of which seven are visible to the naked eye), 430 light years away from the Sun in the constellation of Taurus.

In all, between January 1975 and April 1978, Meier met five Pleiadians – Semjase, Ptaah, Quetzal, Plaja and Asket – in 105 encounters, photographed their five different types of flying disk on numerous occasions, and took 3000 pages of notes on their conversations and general wisdom. According to Meier, the Pleiadians look like terrestrial Scandinavians, although their lifespan stretches to the equivalent of 1000 of our years. They came from a planet named Erra 'in the system of Taygeta' in the Pleiades, and before that from a planet in the constellation of Lyra, from which they had emigrated millions of years previously. They had reached Earth thousands of years ago, as part of a continuous programme of space exploration, in ships capable of travelling faster than light through 'hyperspace'. Their general message for mankind was that we should concentrate on the arts of peace and cultivating the life of the spirit – otherwise, Earth was 'an insane society rushing headlong to our own destruction'. The Pleiadians communicated with Meier both through telepathy and by speaking his own dialect.

By astronomical standards, the Pleiades is young: a mere 150 million years old. Its 500-odd stars are virtually all 'B' type – ferociously hot, very large blue stars that burn themselves out very rapidly – most, in fact, have already consumed most of the hydrogen in their cores. In contrast, our Sun, a relatively cool, slow-burning 'G2' yellow dwarf, is some 4.49 billion years old, and it took a further 2.5 billion years or so before conditions on Earth were able to support even the most primitive forms of life. The chances that any planet in the Pleiades is habitable are about zero.

Above: ***Eduard 'Billy' Meier, the one-armed Swiss farmer who claimed to have had hundreds of contacts with cosmonauts from the Pleiades star cluster in the mid to late 1970s. The picture on the wall behind him, he claims, is of the Pleiadian Semjase.***

Assuming that extra-terrestrial entities of some kind did make contact with Meier, one can only conclude that they were lying about their present galactic address. The obvious question is: why? And if they lie about that, why should we take anything else they say seriously?

The claims made by the aliens in the Meier case are as incredible as those in another, almost equidistant in time between Adamski's encounter in California and the events in Switzerland, that occurred in New York State. On 24 April 1964, farmer Gary Wilcox of Newark Valley, Tioga County, noticed something shiny about 800 yds away, among some trees on a hill where he was working. He drove his tractor up the hill, dismounted, and approached a cigar-shaped object, that was hovering just off the ground.

Wilcox kicked it. It felt, he said, like metallic canvas. Then, out from under it, came two 4 ft tall but otherwise featureless creatures who, in the conversation that followed, claimed to be Martians. After an innocent conversation in which the two entities made two predictions that turned out not to be true (one foretold the death of astronaut John Glenn within the year), they departed in their noiseless, 20 ft long craft. This occurred at a time when no space

facets of ufology is the frequency with which these occur. The veteran ufologist and former editor of the internationally respected journal *Flying Saucer Review*, the late Charles Bowen, once offered his readers a few of the choice messages that ufonauts offer to witnesses.

For instance, in 1968 two beings with transparent legs handed an Argentinian farmer's son a written message that translated as 'You shall know the world' and was signed 'F. Saucer'. In 1964, a Venezuelan contactee, confronted by a pair of creatures who were hardly inconspicuous, in that they stood between 7 and 8 ft tall and sported long yellow hair and bulging eyes, asked – with commendable wit, in the circumstances – if any other 'human beings' like them were living on Earth. The reply was 'Yes. Two million, four hundred and seventeen thousand, eight hundred and five.'

Above: ***Walter H. Andrus Jr, who has analysed thousands of 'alien visitor' reports and detected a number of recurrent patterns within them.***

Right: ***An artist's impression of an encounter with ufonauts that occurred near Cennina, Arezzo, Italy, on 1 November 1954. Note the craft – few real UFO encounters conform to the 'flying saucer with little green men' stereotype.***

scientist believed that any life form more complex than bacteria might be able to survive in Martian conditions.

THE MESSAGE WAS SIGNED 'F. SAUCER'.

VOLUPTUOUS FORMS

These contacts were elaborate and detailed for those who experienced them. They also contain elements of absurdity, illogic and falsehood on the part of the interstellar visitors, but one of the more surprising

Perhaps the most surreal of these utterances came in 1954, when a Frenchman came across a glowing, saucer-shaped UFO, in front of which was standing a diminutive entity who kept repeating, in a mechanical tone: *'La verité est refusée aux constipés'* ('Truth is denied to the constipated'), and *'Ce que vous appelez le cancer vient des dents'* ('What you call cancer comes from the teeth').

If these beings, who seem habitually to

lie about their origins and occasionally make obscurely hilarious observations to the humans they meet, are indeed aliens visiting Earth from other planets, one would expect some consistency at least in their appearance. In fact, they take many more forms than the voluptuous young man who greeted Adamski, or the shapely Nordic blondes of Meier's acquaintance. And they are by no means as friendly or concerned for our welfare as the beings that Adamski and Meier met.

A HEADLESS FIGURE

Walter Andrus, director of the Mutual UFO Network, studied thousands of contactee cases and concluded that there were four major categories of UFO occupants. These were: small humanoids; 'experimental animals'; human-like entities; and robots. ('Little green men', the staple mocking term of the media, however, are hardly ever seen in real UFO contacts.) But these broad categories blur a multitude of differences found from one witness's report to the next.

The term 'human-like entities' encompasses extremes as far apart as the two gigantic beings seen filling a sphere as tall as a two-storey house over the Canary Islands on 22 June 1976; the blue, scaly-skinned, 6 ft tall creature that confronted 19-year-old Maria Eliada Pretzel in Córdoba, Argentina, on 13 June 1968; the creature inside a UFO seen by William Bosak near Frederic, Wisconsin, in December 1974 that had a tan-coloured, furry body, a flat nose and mouth, protruding eyes and 'calf-like' ears; and the truly nightmarish creature that in November 1976 emerged from a UFO near Winchester, England, and stared into a car in which Joyce Bowles and Terry Pratt sat in terror: the thing was human in all visible details but for its eyes, which were entirely pink, with neither irises nor pupils, and luminescent.

The animal forms can be unexpectedly horrible. In 1960, during a UFO sighting at Yssandon, France, giant white maggots were seen crawling across a road. On 16 November 1963, two couples walking near Sandling Park in Saltwood, Kent, saw a bright golden oval UFO come down from the sky and then hover among some trees nearby. A figure emerged and approached them, but the foursome fled when it was close enough for them to make out its features: it was entirely black, had wings like a bat, and no head.

Perhaps the most common form taken by UFO occupants is the classic 'small humanoid' – figures on which Steven Spielberg based both 'ET' and the creatures seen emerging from the giant spaceship in *Close Encounters of the Third Kind* (for which Spielberg used the late Dr J. Allen Hynek, a global authority on UFOs who invented the title phrase, as a consultant). Even these pale, huge-headed, hairless, soft-eyed and innocent-looking entities, which so much resemble human foetuses, vary enormously in detail, according to the witnesses' reports.

They may stand from 1 to 5 ft in height. Their eyes may be like ours, or slitted, like a cat's. Sometimes they appear apparently naked; at other times in shiny black, yellow or blue garb, possibly with a cloak. Some have pointy ears, others none. Betty and Barney Hill, of New Hampshire, believed that in 1961 they had been taken aboard a craft belonging to such creatures (who were clothed in black) and given medical examinations; while in August 1990, five such beings, of various heights, apparently without clothes and with grey skin, and

THEY BELIEVED THE NIGHTMARISH CREATURE WAS HUMAN UNTIL THEY LOOKED INTO ITS EYES.

Below: ***Steven Spielberg, creator of 'ET' and director of the hit movie*** **Close Encounters of the Third Kind.** ***The film was the first to show a wide audience the alien forms most often reported by witnesses. But, while Spielberg's films show aliens as essentially friendly, many actual encounters have been with creatures that were both hostile and dangerous.***

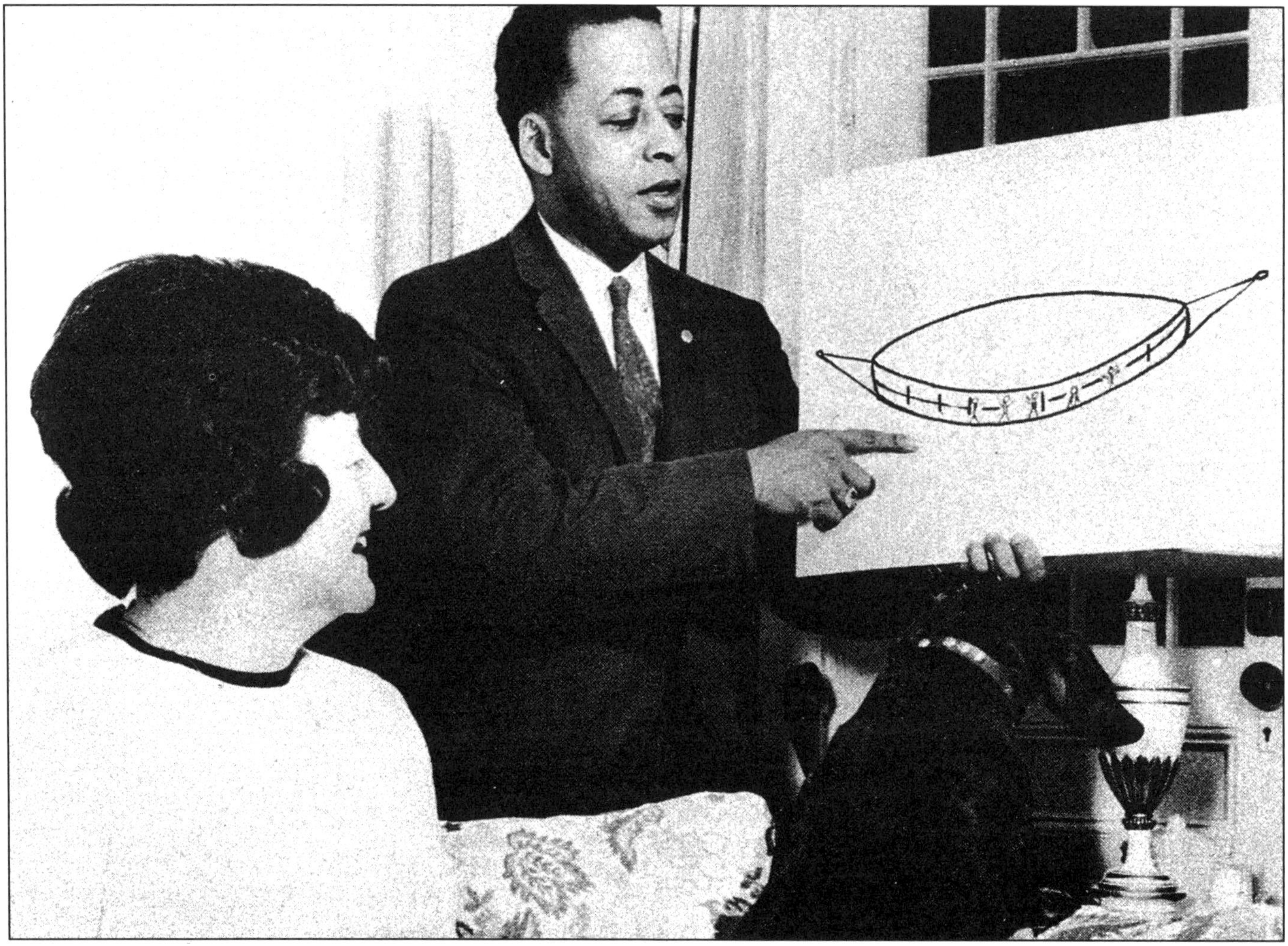

Above: ***Betty and Barney Hill, whose abduction aboard a UFO in 1961 has been the subject of innumerable analyses. None has entirely explained what the couple experienced, or why they were apparently chosen for an alien experiment.***

THE ALIENS ARE DELIBERATELY CONTROLLING THE MINDS OF THE WITNESSES TO PREVENT US LEARNING THEIR TRUE INTENTIONS.

with only three toes on each foot, were seen walking along a main highway in Puerto Rico by numerous witnesses, but made no attempt to molest anyone. These did have the virtue of slightly resembling the creatures seen at Rio Piѐdras, Puerto Rico, on 3 March 1980, when teenagers Vivian and José Rodriguez surprised two pointy-eared creatures who were clothed, and had webbed feet.

On other occasions, such creatures have paralysed witnesses with lightbeams from their craft – or their eyes – or physically attacked people in daylight. In the hair-raising episode experienced by Lorenzo Flores and Jesús Gómez near Carora, Venezuela, on 10 December 1954, a band of humanoids tried to drag Gómez away until his companion retaliated with his shotgun (the pair were on a hunting trip).

Most bizarre of all the perceived occupants of UFOs have been the so-called robot figures, and possibly the weirdest of all was reported by Jerry Townsend, a radio station employee from Minnesota. On the evening of 23 October 1965 he was driving toward Long Prairie when his car's electrical systems went totally dead and the engine stopped. In front him on the road was a V-2-style 'spaceship', between 30 and 35 ft tall and resting on the tips of three fins, that might have featured in any 1950s sci-fi movie. Undaunted, Townsend got out of the car to investigate and saw, coming from beneath the rocket, three ludicrous objects walking towards him. They were no more than 6 in tall, reeling like drunken sailors on two fins, and shaped like beer cans. When they halted, a third, rear fin descended to keep them upright. In due course they tottered back to their antiquated 'rocket' and it took off – which part of the incident was also witnessed by two hunters who were some distance away.

MIND CONTROL

None of this catalogue of strangeness – which only scrapes the surface of the cases on file – suggests that the being that was

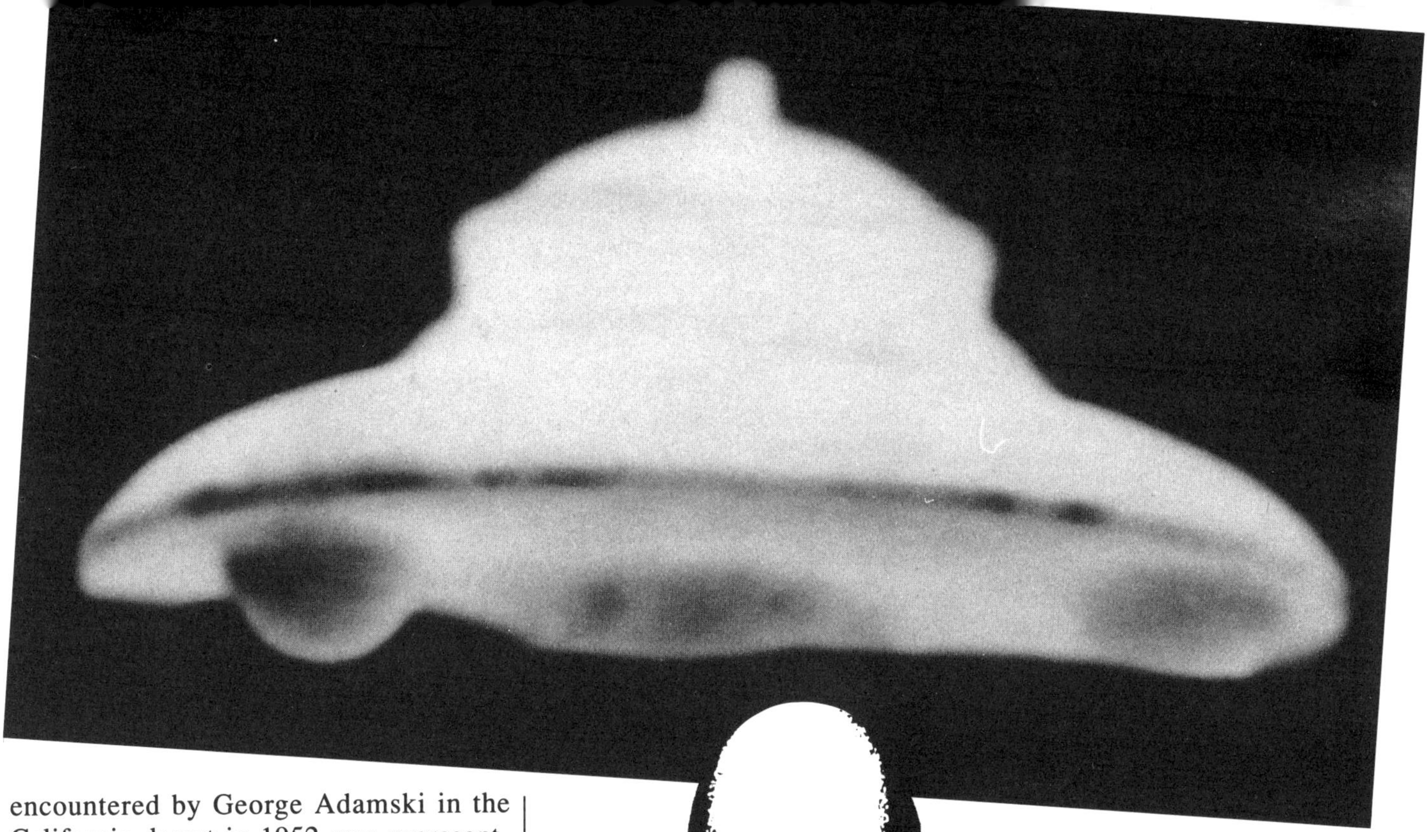

encountered by George Adamski in the California desert in 1952 was representative of its type. The brutal fact is that there is no 'type' at all when one is dealing with UFO entities, and no general conclusion to be drawn from the available evidence about their intentions and still less where they come from. So what are they?

Ufologist and specialist in radiation medicine Maxwell C. Cade once suggested that UFO occupants deliberately monitored, and reflected, what was in the mind of the witness: in some cases, homing in on their fears. Thus, the sceptics' dismissal of the contactee phenomenon that 'It's all hallucination' may be true, but with a significant and unexpected twist. According to Cade's hypothesis, the hallucinations are generated *from within the UFO*, not directly by the witness.

This would explain the huge variations in the degree of sympathy or hostility that contactees encounter among aliens, as well as the bewildering variety of shapes, sizes, colours and textures the entities display. And it would also explain the quality of alien behaviour so shrewdly noted by ufologist Peter Hough – that they 'act less like "aliens" than as if they are fledgling temporary beings hastily assembled and scripted to act out a brief scenario'.

If Cade's hypothesis is correct, it has a clear corollary: whatever they are and wherever they are from, the occupants of UFOs are doing everything in their power to prevent us seeing their true forms or learning their real intentions.

'Typical' flying saucers and alien figures, like these, in fact make up a minority of real UFO encounter reports. Both the craft and their mysterious occupants vary enormously in size, shape, and colour – and in the ufonauts' actions and statements, which range from the amiably banal to the savage and depraved.

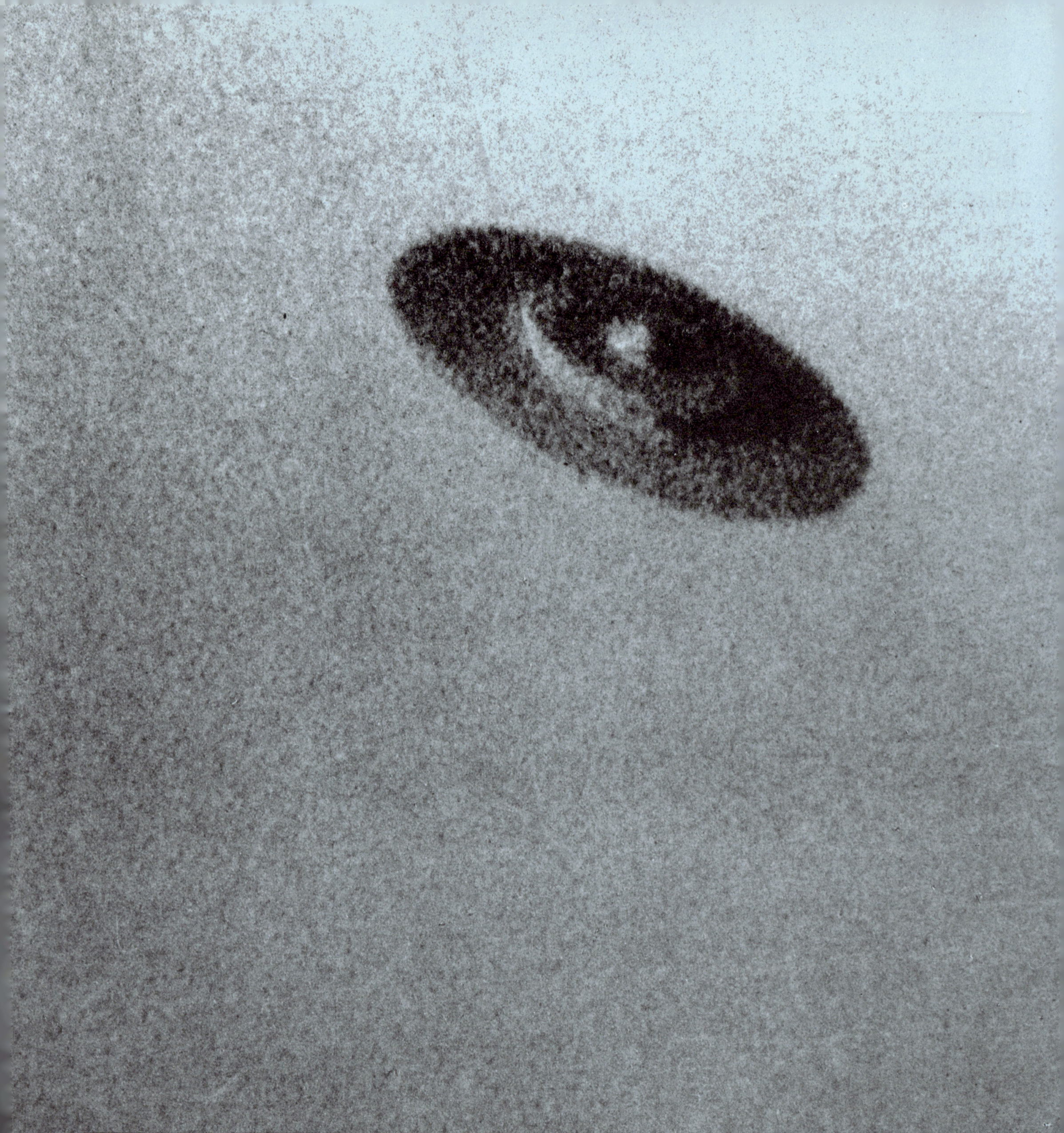

ENCOUNTERS WITH THE UNKNOWN

There have now been so many close encounters with UFO phenomena that it is very hard to deny their existence. Terrible injuries have been inflicted on some of the witnesses – but were these encounters with rogue military hardware, or with alien craft on a mission?

Dr J. Allen Hynek (1910–86) was one of the most dedicated, and one of the best-informed, of ufologists the world has seen. A professional astronomer, long a professor, and in due course head of the astronomy department at North Western University in Evanston, Illinois (a suburb of Chicago), Hynek was also one of those fortunate beings who always happen to be in the right place at the right time. In the late 1940s, when still in his early thirties, Hynek was recognized as a rising star (so to speak) and appointed astronomical consultant to the USAF's Project Sign, the official – if not the only – government body established to gather and assess UFO reports. Sign collapsed in 1949, its belief in

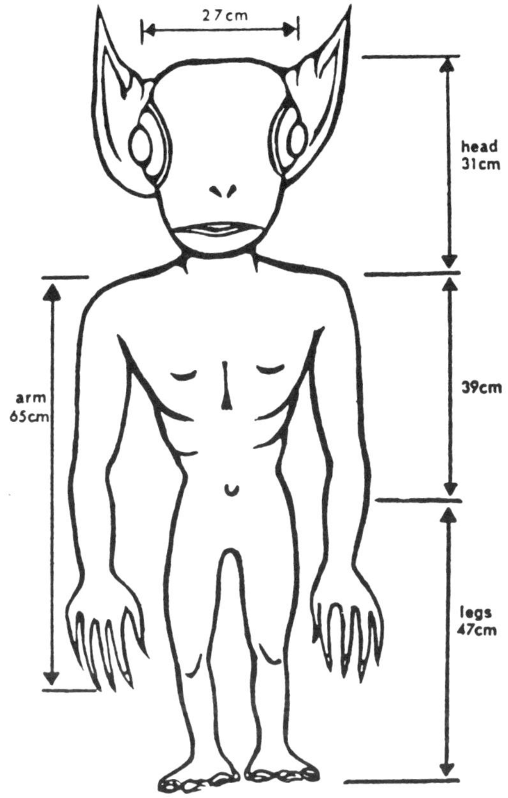

EVENTUALLY THE FAMOUS PROFESSOR WAS FORCED TO CONCEDE THAT SOME CLOSE ENCOUNTERS WITH ALIENS WERE POSSIBLY GENUINE.

Opposite: ***This daylight disk was allegedly photographed from an aircraft at Barra da Tijuca, Brazil, on 7 May 1952. South America has always been a rich source of UFO reports, some of them of the most intriguing kind.***

Left: ***A diagrammatic representation of one of the goblin-like entities that besieged the Sutton farm at Kelly, near Hopkinsville, Kentucky, in August 1955. The creatures were impervious to gunfire, and persisted in terrorizing the Sutton family through an entire night, although their purpose in doing so never became clear.***

Below left: ***Dr J. Allen Hynek, the professor of astronomy whose tireless efforts did much to put UFO studies on a scientific basis. Hynek began analysing UFO reports at the behest of the US Air Force in the late 1940s, and did so at first as a sceptic. The nature of the evidence and the integrity of the overwhelming majority of witnesses soon convinced him that something real lay behind the UFO enigma.***

Above: ***Proof of alien contact and government cover-up – this picture, taken in Germany in the 1950s, shows a tiny alien corpse from a saucer that had crashed near Mexico City and had been sent to Europe for analysis. That, at least, was what many UFO buffs believed, until assiduous research showed that the picture was first seen in an April Fools' edition of a German student magazine in the early 1970s.***

the extra-terrestrial origins of UFOs disbelieved and savagely discredited by the USAF establishment, to be succeeded by Project Grudge and in due course by the longstanding Project Blue Book, which was eventually wound up in 1969.

Hynek survived these political shifts and upheavals, and remained a USAF consultant right through until the end of Project Blue Book, when the USAF officially proclaimed the end of its interest in UFOs. Always, from his earliest professional acquaintance with UFOs until his dying day, Hynek rejected the extra-terrestrial hypothesis – the belief that UFOs and their occupants come from some reach of space beyond this Earth – but in the course of 20 years spent investigating UFO reports on behalf of the USAF came to be convinced that something indubitably real lay behind the UFO phenomenon.

In 1984, in a brief survey of the subject, Hynek summed up his own belief concerning UFOs as follows:

'It is far from certain that UFOs represent a single phenomenon, despite the similarity in patterns of reports from all over the world...Perhaps I may presume to intrude my own opinion on these matters, based on more than 30 years of study. I believe that the UFO phenomenon is in some way directing us to consider an aspect of reality of which we have been hitherto largely unaware – an aspect, indeed, that may eventually be incorporated into our science and may prove to be of great value to the progress of mankind.'

During the International Symposium of the Center for UFO Studies (of which he was founder and director) in Chicago in 1981, Hynek confided to the author of this book that he believed that UFOs were directed by some kind of intelligence. 'That intelligence may be our own,' he added, but did not expand on his conclusion. Perhaps he felt he did not have to.

CLOSE ENCOUNTERS

So far in this survey of the UFO phenomenon, we have seen that while there is little doubt that the phenomenon itself is real, the hard evidence that it is a physical reality is singularly elusive. The proof, in the form of a solid and indisputable example of a grounded UFO or a captured alien, does not exist. Nevertheless, UFOs of considerable size, apparent complexity and the ability to affect the environment around them continue to be seen and reported. How should one start to sort this kind of evidence?

One of Hynek's most useful contributions to the often confused debate about UFOs was a scheme for analysing the evidence: a standard and non-controversial classification of UFO sightings that any interested party could use as a starting point from which to approach the subject. Hynek divided UFO reports into two basic categories, 'distant' sightings and 'close' encounters. 'Distant' meant that the perceived object was further than 500 ft from the observer; a 'close' encounter is one that takes place less than 500 ft away from the witness.

Under distant sightings he listed three sub-categories:

(1) Nocturnal lights – which qualify as UFOs when they make unusual manoeuvres, change speed or direction, show unorthodox configurations, colours or

intensity of lights, in such a way as to rule out the presence of conventional aircraft or natural phenomena.

(2) Daylight disks – unusual flying objects seen in daylight. Their shapes may be like cigars, spheres, triangles, boomerangs, eggs, and even pinpoints.

(3) Radar visuals – a comparatively rare event, when there is instrumental evidence of an unidentified object that correlates with the witness's 'subjective' report. Hynek rejected UFOs detected solely by radar because of the high proportion of 'clutter' that can appear on radar screens, especially those scanning near ground level. This distinction has perhaps become less important since many aircraft, civil and military, are now equipped with transponders that identify them individually on air traffic control and military radar screens. A consistent 'unknown' appearing in commercial or military airspace with no such electronic tag may well be a UFO.

Hynek also listed three 'kinds' of close encounter:

(1) Close encounters of the first kind: UFOs are witnessed at close quarters but do not affect the environment.

(2) Close encounters of the second kind: the UFO has physical effects on animate and/or inanimate objects around it –

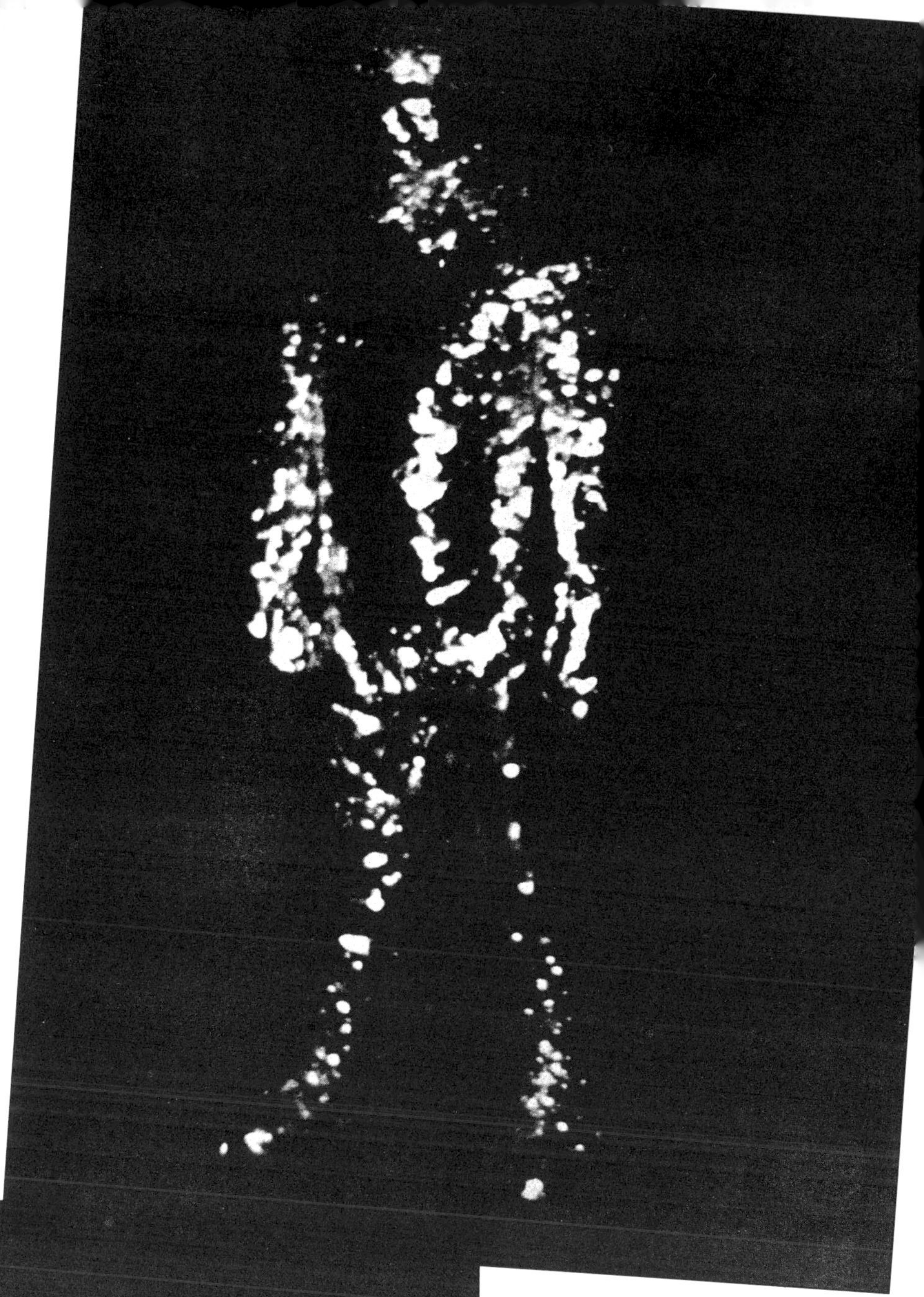

Above: ***The bizarre silver-suited creature that Jeff Greenshaw, police chief of Falkville, Alabama, encountered on 17 October 1973.***

Left: ***According to engineer Paul Paulin, who took this picture of a UFO over Paris at around 3.45 am on 29 December 1953, the craft remained stationary long enough for him to set up a 2-minute time exposure on his camera. During the exposure, the light leapt to a fresh position.***

animals are frightened, the ground is burned, electromagnetic systems such as radios or car lights and engines cease to function, and so on.

(3) Close encounters of the third kind: entities are seen in or near the UFO. Initially Hynek rejected reports that people had had intelligent communication with the occupants of UFOs, and reports of abductions, as never being made by 'sensible, rational and reputable persons' but did come to accept some experiences of this kind. Such cases are now often referred to as 'Close encounters of the fourth kind' in deference to the fact that his system of classification has now become standard among UFO analysts.

Hynek also referred to some UFO reports as having 'high strangeness', although he never made this term part of his system of ordering as such.

THE BLACK SQUADRON

The nocturnal light is the most commonly reported UFO and is the sighting most prone to misidentification, wishful thinking or even, in extreme cases, fantasy. The number of advertising planes, their sides ablaze with some promotional message, is legion in the USA, and so is the number that have been proved to be the source of the most authentic-sounding UFO reports.

***Close encounters of the third kind, as shown in artist's impressions – a meeting between a French farmer, two entities and their egg-shaped craft in a lavender field in the 1950s* (above), *and aliens seen apparently repairing their spherical craft in northern Italy* (below).**

Even the most orthodox aircraft, seen at night at an unexpected angle, especially if it is large and replete with tail illuminations, landing lamps and anti-collision beacons, can become a veritable festival of light – and look very strange indeed.

Daylight disks – unless the sighting is supported by high-quality photographs – can be equally ambiguous. The editor of the British partwork magazine *The Unexplained* once recounted how in the late 1970s he had been driving the sparsely travelled US Route 95 between Beatty and Las Vegas, Nevada, when around mid-afternoon he saw streaking across the sky an object that looked like no aircraft known to him (the son of an aviation engineer and inventor, he is familiar with a wide range of aircraft).

The craft performed no bizarre manoeuvres or aerobatics, but it was oval shaped, with a slight bulge at the rear end, apparently wingless and tailless, and 'the color of dried blood'. Its speed was 'no greater than might be expected from a large, fast strike aircraft – say an F-15 Eagle – at that apparent distance'. That would by most standards be very fast – the F-15 can top 1800 mph in level flight. But there was in any case no way of knowing whether the mystery object was very small and very near, or very large and very distant; the featureless desert terrain was no help in deciding how far away the craft was, or in giving some clue as to its real

size. But he was intrigued to find himself, some miles further on, passing the entrance to the USAF's Indian Springs base. Such installations seem to attract UFOs.

As it happened, the witness soon had a clue to what he may have seen: returning to Phoenix, Arizona, where he was the guest of a former USAF pilot, he learned that Indian Springs is indeed out of the usual run of USAF bases: it is the home of the USAF's 'black squadron' of covertly acquired Soviet aircraft, and over the years has been host to a number of experimental aircraft. The apparent size and, most particularly, the wingless shape and unusual colour of the object he had seen matched that of an aerofoil designed and built by NASA as part of its development programme for the space shuttle. The first shuttle was launched about a year after this sighting, so why a one-off experimental craft should still be flying, in such a location, so late in the life of NASA's programme is anyone's guess. But the point of this account was to illustrate the ambiguous nature of daylight disk sightings – even partly explained ones!

HIDDEN PURPOSES

Radar/visual cases, when they occur, offer much richer pickings to the ufologist, but they still offer no clear-cut clues as to the nature of what has caused the sighting, or what the purpose of the UFO may have been at the time.

At around 9 pm on 10 October 1990, residents around Skibo, Minnesota, began reporting unusual lights in the sky that were appearing to the south-east of nearby Hoyt Lakes. Two police officers who were sent to investigate saw, as did other witnesses, numerous objects 'of indeterminate shape, alternately hovering and darting about'. A little over an hour after the first reports were received, the Federal Aviation Authority's air traffic controllers at Duluth, the area's major airport, confirmed radar echoes from the Hoyt

*Military fast-movers (***below:** *the McDonnell Douglas F-15 Eagle) and experimental craft from civilian programmes such as the NASA space shuttle* **(right)** *may easily be taken for UFOs by witnesses unfamiliar with the shapes of such machines. High speed and high manoeuvrability also give an 'alien' impression, as a staff member of the magazine* **The Unexplained (above)** *found in the Nevada desert in the late 1970s.*

JUST WHAT KIND OF BIZARRE REALITY ARE WE DEALING WITH?

Lakes area, and for more than an hour after that one of the ATCs at Duluth monitored the echoes. There were between three and five objects registering intermittently, in a roughly circular formation. The local National Air Guard radar also picked up the same returns.

Further confirmation came from the pilot of a commercial aircraft flying at 11,000 ft about 45 miles west of Hoyt Lakes, who reported seeing two steady, distinct, and unidentified lights at an estimated 1000 ft below him. They were a few miles apart and a deep, glowing red. Investigators noted that no other conventional aircraft were in the area, and 'no known weather factors accounted for the anomalous radar returns'.

Below: ***Patrolman Lonnie Zamora of the Socorro, New Mexico, city police, whose close encounter in 1964 has become a classic of ufology.***

HARD EVIDENCE

The most spectacular UFO cases are without doubt the 'close encounters', and it is in these, especially in encounters of the second kind, that we might best be able to judge whether Hynek was on to something in speculating that the UFO phenomenon is 'in some way directing us to an aspect of reality of which we have hitherto been largely unaware'. For here, the normal and the paranormal seem to meet at an interface – as they do to a lesser extent in radar/visual cases, but as they do not in the almost wholly paranormal and possibly entirely psychological experiences that constitute close encounters of the third kind.

This is not to say that something real does not happen in such encounters, but they are one crucial stage further removed from the everyday material world than those of the second kind. And this makes encounters of the third kind exceptionally difficult to analyse, for we are again, immediately, confronted with the old riddle about the *kind* of reality we are dealing with. In close encounters of the second kind we have at least a modicum of 'hard' evidence to add to the witnesses' accounts of their subjective experience. Hynek himself said close encounters of the second kind 'bear a special importance, for when it is reported that a UFO left tangible evidence of its presence...we find the real challenge to scientific enquiry'.

RED INSIGNIA

One of the classic such cases occurred at Socorro, New Mexico, in 1964 – the same town near which, in 1947, Grady L. Barnett reputedly found a crashed UFO. At about 5.45 pm on 24 April 1964 – a clear, sunny day with a strong wind blowing – patrolman Lonnie Zamora, on duty in the Socorro Two police cruiser, gave chase to a speeding Chevrolet. Whilst in pursuit, he heard a brief roar and saw a flame in the sky to his right. Zamora knew there was a shack containing dynamite in the vicinity, and his first thought was that it had blown up. He abandoned his chase and headed for the shack.

During this time the flame – blue and orange in colour, smokeless, long and narrow, and broadening toward the bottom

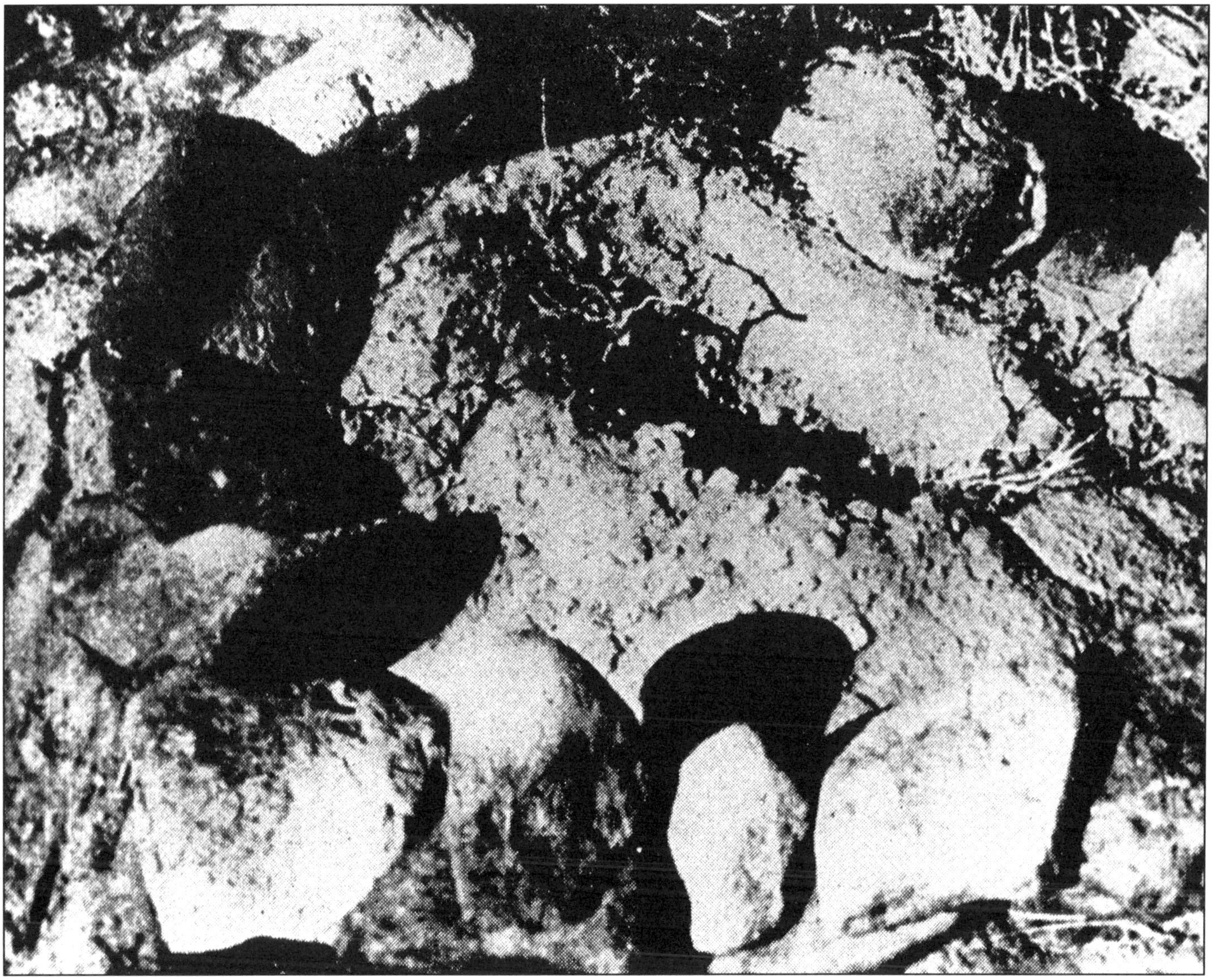

– was descending toward the ground. The base of the flame was invisible behind a low hill to Zamora's left. Concentrating on his driving, he did not notice any object atop the flame and, besides, the sun was in his eyes.

While looking out for the shack, he noticed 'a shiny type object to [the] south' between 100 and 200 yds off the road and below him in a gully. 'It looked,' Zamora told FBI agent J. Arthur Byrnes Jr later the same day, 'like a car turned upside down...standing on [its] radiator or trunk.'

Next to the object were 'two people in white coveralls...One of these persons seemed to turn and look straight at my car and seemed startled – seemed to quickly jump somewhat.' They 'appeared normal in shape – but possibly they were small adults or large kids'. Zamora radioed Sgt Sam Chavez at the sheriff's office in Socorro that he was about to investigate a possible accident, then, as he got out of the car, his radio mike fell. While he turned back to replace it, he heard 'two or three loud thumps...a second or less apart'.

Zamora approached to within 75 or 100 ft of the object, which he now saw was oval and smooth, with no windows or doors, on girder-like legs. He also noted red insignia on its side, about 2 1/2 ft wide. Then the roar began again, low frequency at first, rising rapidly and getting 'very loud'. The object was emitting a flame and kicking up dust. There was no sign of the 'persons' he had seen before.

Zamora thought the object might explode, and ran. The roar stopped, and he looked back to see the UFO 'going away from me in a south-west direction... possibly 10 to 15 ft above the ground, and it cleared the dynamite shack by about 3 ft'. The UFO, now travelling very fast but no longer emitting either noise or

Above: ***A 'footprint' left on the desert terrain by one of the stabilizer struts of the Socorro UFO. Stones were placed around the mark to protect it.***

Above: ***Another of the traces left by the Socorro UFO. The depth of the impression suggested that the mystery craft weighed at least 4 tons.***

flame, rose up and sped away. It 'just cleared' a mountain in the distance and disappeared.

When Sgt Chavez arrived on the scene, he and Zamora went to investigate the spot where the UFO had landed, and where the brush was still burning. They were soon joined by FBI Agent Byrne, in Socorro on another case – and Deputy Sheriff James Lucky. They found four burn marks, and four V-shaped depressions, between 1 and 2 in deep and roughly 18 in long, in the ground in an asymmetrical diamond pattern around the burns. These corresponded to the 'legs' Zamora had seen on the mystery craft, and an independent engineer's analysis later declared that each would have been bearing a load of at least 1 ton to press so deeply into the dense earth of the district. Five other, smaller marks nearby were labelled 'footprints'. All these marks were photographed the following day.

Hynek arrived in Socorro on 28 April to investigate the sighting on behalf of the USAF's Project Blue Book. His first task was to establish the truth of Zamora's testimony, and that he could not fault. At his instigation, the USAF checked – to no avail – if any aerospace company had been privately developing such a craft. The USAF did not, however, follow up Hynek's request that they attempt to trace the car driver who told the manager of a gas station on US Highway 85 (since superseded by Interstate 25) that he had seen some kind of aircraft just south of town, obviously in trouble and landing – and a police car was approaching it.

Sceptics have had some difficulty in trying to dispose of the Socorro case, imputing motives for a hoax to the town's mayor and suggesting that otherwise Zamora saw a 'ball of plasma' and imagined the rest. The USAF initially thought that a lunar exploration module, then being developed, was somehow responsible, but no such vehicle resembles what Zamora saw; Blue Book finally classified the sighting as 'unidentified'. Hynek himself concluded that 'a real physical event' occurred in Socorro that day.

HYSTERICAL WITH FEAR

A less celebrated but no less intriguing case occurred in England three and a half years after the events at Socorro. Sometime between 1 and 2 am on 6 November 1967, Carl Farlow was driving his truck on the A338 trunk road between the villages of Sopley and Avon in Hampshire. He was approaching a junction when his lights died. The truck's diesel engine (which does not depend on an electrical ignition system) kept running and, assuming a simple short-circuit of some kind, Farlow pulled up to investigate.

Before he could climb down from the cab, he was astonished to see a bizarre egg-shaped object move from right to left across the road in front of him at about 25 ft from the ground. It was magenta coloured, with a white base, and was perhaps 80 ft long – big enough to overhang both sides of the road as it passed, exuded a smell 'like a drill boring through wood' and made a sound 'like a refrigerator'. As it crossed the road it accelerated gradually, then disappeared.

Farlow then realized that a Jaguar sedan, which had been coming in the opposite direction, was stranded on the other side of the UFO's path. Its driver, who was a veterinarian, approached Farlow, explained that his vehicle was out of action and his lady passenger hysterical, and suggested they call the police. The police arrived at the scene shortly afterwards. Their preliminary inspection of the site showed that the surface of the road seemed to have melted. The vet's passenger was taken to hospital to be treated for shock, while the two men were questioned first by police and later by a member of the Ministry of Defence.

Next day, Farlow returned to his truck. A bulldozer was at work levelling the road, the phone booth was being repainted, and other people seemed to be investigating the area with instruments. A week or so later, taking the same route in his truck, Farlow saw that some 70 yds of that particular stretch of road had been resurfaced.

BURNT BY RADIATION

Betty Cash, Vickie Landrum and her 7-year-old grandson Colby Landrum were driving home to Dayton, near Houston, Texas, on the evening of 29 December 1980, after a meal in nearby New Caney. Around 9 pm the trio, with Betty at the

Below: ***One of the most baffling, bizarre and frightening of modern UFO cases – the 'Cash-Landrum' encounter near Huffman, Texas, in 1980, which left the witnesses suffering all the symptoms of radiation poisoning and appeared to involve the US military.***

THE THREE VICTIMS SUFFERED TERRIBLE SIDE-EFFECTS AFTER THEIR EXPOSURE TO THE STRANGE ELECTROMAGNETIC RADIATION.

wheel, were on Highway FM1485, which runs through a forest of oak and pine. Then, Colby pointed to a bright light moving over the trees ahead of them. The light grew larger and larger – until it became 'like a diamond of fire', in Vickie Landrum's words – while every so often flames burst from beneath it. Suddenly, it was right in their way.

Betty braked hard. The three watched as the UFO hovered above the road about 60 yds away. From treetop level it sank to within 25 ft of the highway, gave out a blast of fire, and rose again. It did this several times, mesmerizing the car's occupants. They actually climbed out to see the object, which was lighting up the trees and the highway all around it, more clearly. It seemed to be made of dull aluminium, and the four points of its diamond shape were rounded. A row of blue dots ran across its centre. Now and then it emitted a beeping sound. A terrific heat was coming from the UFO, and Colby begged his grandmother to get back in the car. She and he both did, but Betty stayed outside until the object moved up and away. The car was now so hot that she could not touch the door with bare hands. Then a crowd of helicopters

Witnesses' drawings of UFO encounters, one from Lemon Grove, California in 1973 **(right)***; the other from Dyfed, Wales, in 1977* **(opposite)***. The Lemon Grove encounter was certainly with a material object of 'high strangeness' – one of the witnesses actually knocked on the side of the thing with his torch. But the Dyfed case turned out to be the product of a combination of mistaken identity (the 'UFO' was probably a council garbage truck) and a mild form of mass hysteria, which caused many schoolchildren to believe they had seen an alien craft.*

appeared. 'They seemed to rush in from all directions,' said Betty. 'It seemed like they were trying to encircle the thing.'

They drove on another five miles to where they could see the UFO in the distance, and the swarm of helicopters around it. One, a giant, twin-rotor CH-47 Chinook, roared right over them. They counted a total of 23 machines of various types apparently in pursuit of the clearly visible UFO.

But worse was to follow. Over the next few hours, the trio developed painful swellings and blisters on their skin and had severe headaches and stomach upsets. Vickie's hair began to fall out. Colby suffered a sunburn-like rash. Over the following week or so, Betty's eyes also became swollen to the point that she could not see, and she had to be hospitalized. In a few weeks all three had lost some hair and were developing eye problems. Their hair eventually grew again, although it was different from their original hair. Since their experience, none has entirely recovered their former good health. Doctors said that the symptoms shown by the three victims were consistent with exposure to intense electro-magnetic radiation in the ultra-violet, microwave and X-ray bands.

Investigators later established that other witnesses could confirm the UFO's flight path and appearance, and the presence of unusual numbers of CH-47 helicopters – which are quite distinctive – in the sky that night. Yet local civil airfields and military airbases deny that such a fleet used their facilities or showed on their radar. Vickie Landrum was convinced that a secret military device run haywire was responsible for her injuries, and she and Betty Cash sued the US government for $20 million in that belief. In 1986, the case was dismissed on the grounds that 'no such object was owned, operated or in the inventory' of the US Army, Navy, Air Force or NASA.

However, what the US government has *not* said may be significant, for it has not been obliged to admit whether or not it knows what the object was, irrespective of who owns it. So the origin and nature of the Texas UFO – like that of all other UFOs – remains an enigma. That is precious little comfort to those it affected, or to those trying to solve the mystery of UFOs as a whole. The Texas UFO case is

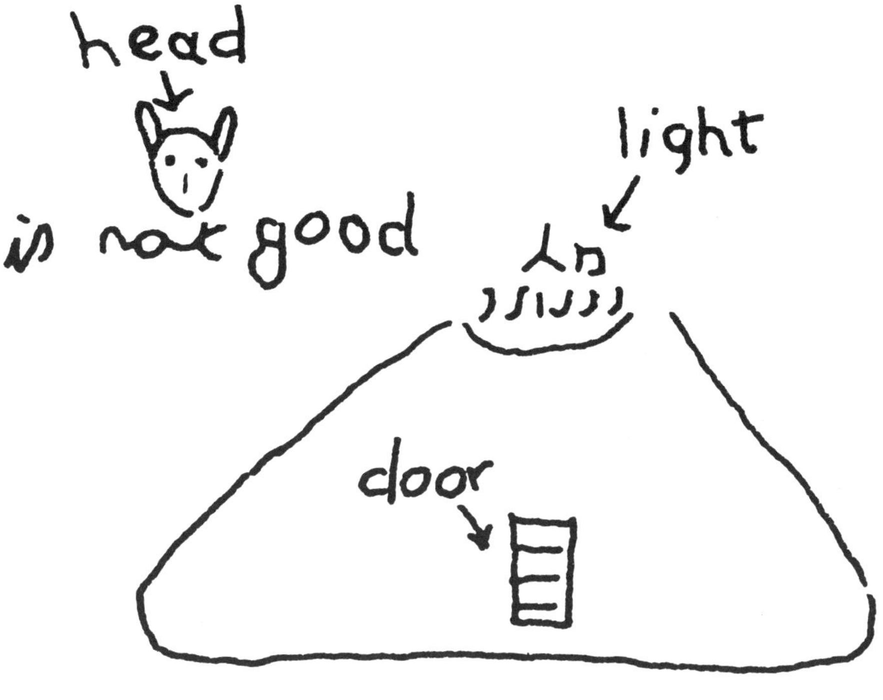

perhaps the most baffling and frustrating of modern times, for what starts with solid evidence for a notoriously elusive phenomenon peters out in a maze of dead ends, official denials, and perhaps even deviousness.

Nonetheless, the three classic close encounters of the second kind discussed here show significant similarities. In the Avon and Texas cases there is a strong indication of military involvement, and it is possible, if by no means proven, that the military may have had some connection with the Socorro case – for by 1964, the White Sands Missile Range had acquired a further 883,910 acres of land that extended the range northwards, east of the town. There are certain physical similarities between the Texas UFO and the Socorro craft. And it is apparent that the authorities had no wish to admit to the existence of either the Avon or the Texas UFO – both of which involved multiple witnesses. And in all cases there were real physical effects, either on people or on the environment.

Are we dealing here with secret military hardware gone wrong, bursting disastrously into public gaze? Or were the UFOs alien craft that were busy trying to escape military scrutiny? Or – the wildest scenario of all, but one that some ufologists take seriously – was the military already well aware that the craft were alien, and simply trying to hide their knowledge, or even their collusion with the UFOs?

SOLID EVIDENCE PETERS OUT IN A MAZE OF DEAD ENDS, UNCONVINCING OFFICIAL DETAILS AND DEVIOUSNESS.

ARE THE MILITARY HIDING – OR EVEN COLLUDING WITH – THE UFOS?

UFOs: THE PHYSICAL EVIDENCE

Evidence of UFOs is dramatic and varied but too often the trail goes cold. Are the scientists being silenced? And, if so, is the controlling force a human mind or something far more powerful?

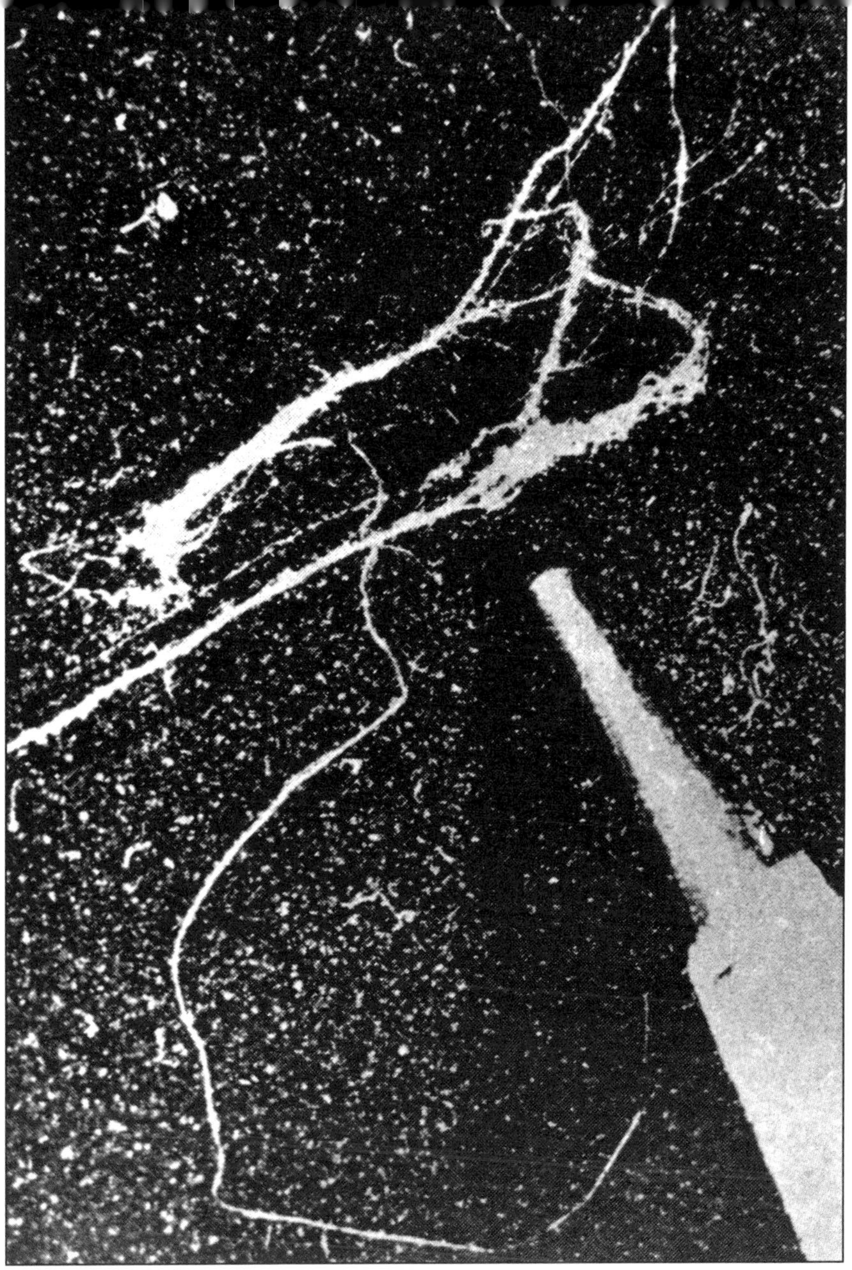

Evidence of UFOs, or a so-far unexplained natural substance? So-called 'angel hair' (**opposite**, *as found in Japan, and* **above**) *has drifted inexplicably from the sky during a significant number of UFO sightings. One of its more curious qualities is its tendency to evaporate, making scientific analysis impossible.*

The three cases considered in the last chapter demonstrate that one part at least of the UFO phenomenon involves actual hardware – since we have to assume that only physical, mechanical objects have the capacity to melt road surfaces, crush compacted, dried-out desert earth, and maim witnesses.

It is also clear from that evidence that these cases do not really illuminate ufologist J. Allen Hynek's remark late in his life that 'the UFO phenomenon is in some way directing us to consider an aspect of reality of which we have been hitherto largely unaware – an aspect, indeed, that may eventually be incorporated into our science and may prove to be of great value to the progress of mankind'. Nor do they bear out his belief that close encounters of the second kind 'bear a special importance, for when it is reported that a UFO left tangible evidence of its presence...we find the real challenge to scientific enquiry'.

For here were three classic close encounters that seem to be all too real in worldly terms to indicate that some other order or aspect of reality is involved (although it may well be in other kinds of encounter, of course). Scientific enquiry bore very little fruit in the two American cases. If it was permitted in the English case, the scientists involved were clearly silenced by the Official Secrets Act. What they already knew, or what they discovered – if anything – is still under wraps.

The manner in which the scientific trail peters out in these cases is typical of the UFO phenomenon as a whole: the most promising clues to at least part of the phenomenon are leads only to dead ends. Even when investigators are presented with quite dramatic evidence, or material that can be put into a laboratory and analysed, the conclusions raise as many questions as they answer. Not the least baffling aspect of the physical traces that UFOs leave behind is that they are as varied as reports of the appearance of UFOs and their extraordinary occupants – as the following, necessarily brief, survey shows.

ANGEL HAIR

French ufologist Aime Michel recounted this instance (of many on record) of the gossamer-like material called 'angel hair' that has occasionally fallen from the sky during a UFO sighting.

At about 12.50 pm on 17 October 1952, a M. Prigent, the headmaster of a school at

WHAT THEY DISCOVERED IS STILL UNDER WRAPS – THE STARTLING REVELATIONS BLOCKED BY THE OFFICIAL SECRETS ACT.

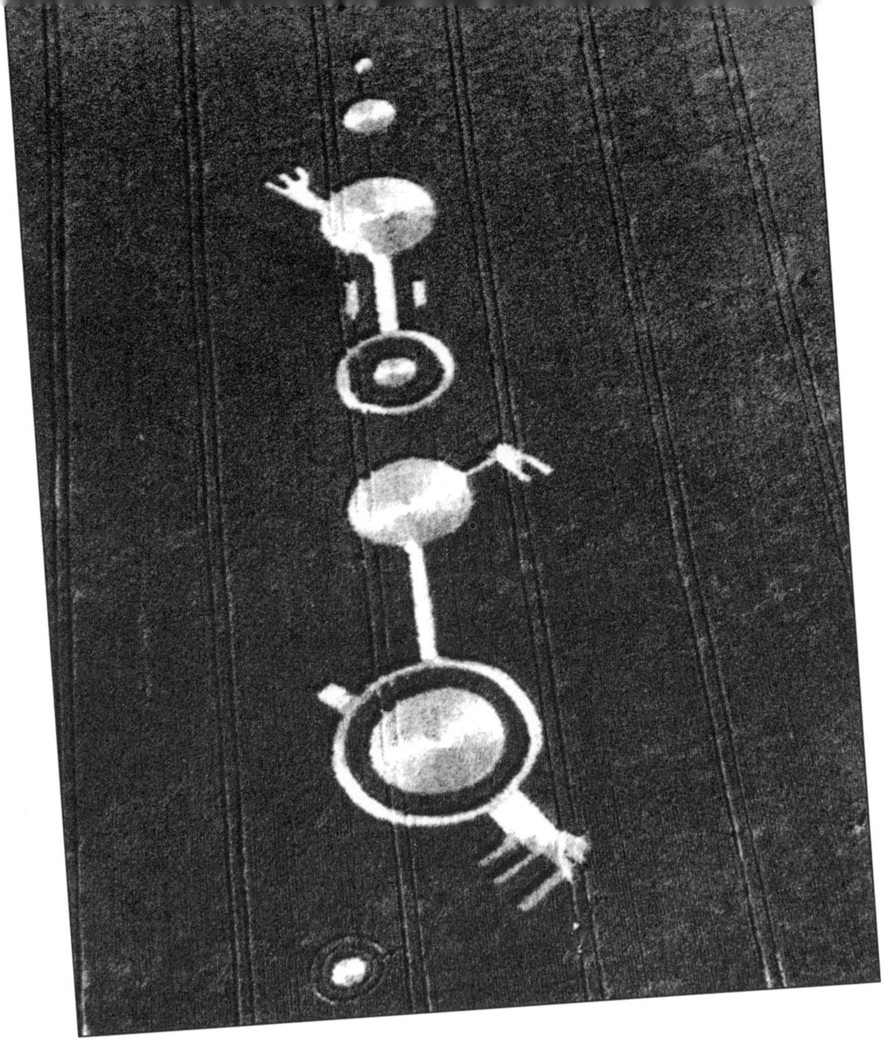

Crop circles **(above)** *were once taken to be UFO 'nests' or landing sites but, unlike the traces found at South Hill, Virginia* **(right and below)***, after a UFO sighting on 21 April 1967, the circles have been shown to be the work of hoaxers or caused by unusual atmospheric conditions.*

Oloron, France, was having lunch with his family when they saw a small fleet of UFOs and a 'mother ship' flying a zigzag course. The latter was a white cylinder, apparently tilted into the sky, at an estimated altitude of 8000 ft. Travelling in pairs ahead of it were some 30 spherical objects that, M. Prigent saw through binoculars, were red spheres with yellow planetary rings around them, like smaller editions of Saturn. From time to time all these objects seemed to give out puffs of smoke, but they also left long trails of some other substance, which drifted to the ground. A large number of witnesses testified that for hours afterwards the material kept falling; it was gelatinous at first, but eventually vaporized and disappeared.

Scientists could offer no clue as to its nature – and, of course, could not examine it.

STEALTH TECHNOLOGY

One of the most dramatic reports of a radar/visual UFO sighting, with radical physical effects as well, hit the Russian press (including the district military newspaper *Za Rodinu*) in 1990, after a series of bizarre events at the long-range radar tracking station near the city of Samara (then called Kuybyshev) in Russia.

At 12.07 am on 13 September 1990, the radar watch saw a blip 'comparable to that of a strategic bomber' at a range of 60 miles appear on their screens. The station's automatic electronic IFF (Identify Friend or Foe) system then failed, preventing the watch from identifying whether the aircraft was hostile or not. Two and a half minutes after its first appearance, the large blip then scattered into a host of smaller returns. By the time these were within 25 miles or so of the station, the largest of them was showing as a triangular-shaped object, and heading straight for the radar post. As it approached, a team of soldiers was scrambled to investigate: the thing shot over their heads, less than 35 ft up, as they came into the open. Then it stopped, hovering about 100 yds beyond a barbed-wire barrier that lay less than 50 yds from a mobile, short-range radar array known as Post No 12. There was a flash, and No 12's paired aerials caught fire; the upper one collapsed to the ground. Later inspection revealed that all the steel parts had been melted.

Many UFO photographs have been shown to be clever fakes, but some have passed the most rigorous computerized tests. Among the latter are those taken by Paul Trent at McMinnville, Oregon, on 11 May 1950 **(above)** *and from a Brazilian Navy research vessel off Trindade Island in the Atlantic on 16 January 1958* **(right).**

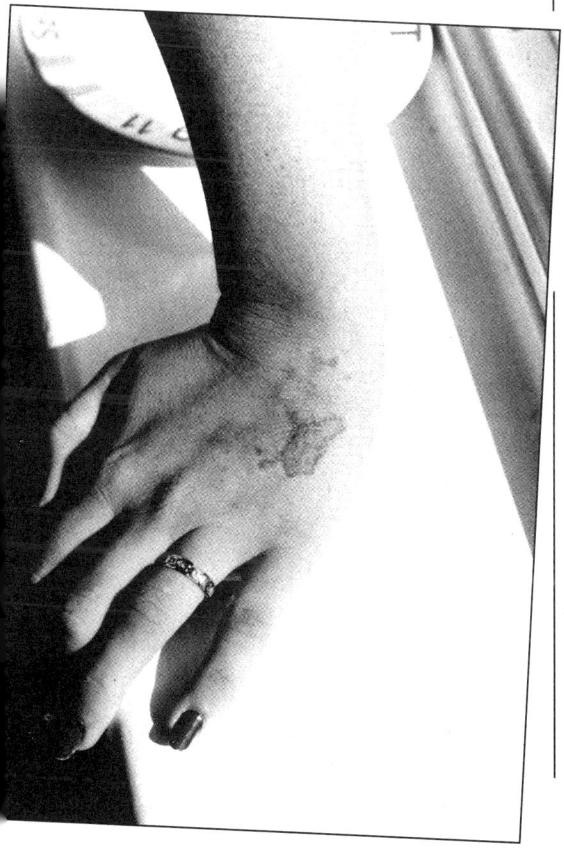

Left: *UFOs may leave physical 'traces' on people as well as on the ground. Here, Denise Bishop displays the effects of her UFO encounter in Plymouth, Devon, on 10 September 1981.*

THE UFO BLOCKED THE ELECTROMAGNETIC DEFENCE SYSTEM AND DESTROYED THE RADAR. THE HELPLESS SOLDIERS COULD DO NOTHING BUT WATCH AND WAIT.

Witnesses – both officers and enlisted men – described the mystery triangle as black and 'smooth...not mirror-like – it was like a thick layer of soot'. Its sides were each about 45 ft long, and it was about 10 ft thick. There were no openings or portholes. The machine remained hovering for about 90 minutes after destroying the radar, while the post soldiers covered it – somewhat optimistically – with small arms. Then it took off.

After the press reports came official denials, and the announcement on 23 September 1990 that the story was a hoax perpetrated by a reporter on *Za Rodinu*. But it seems that a Soviet Defence

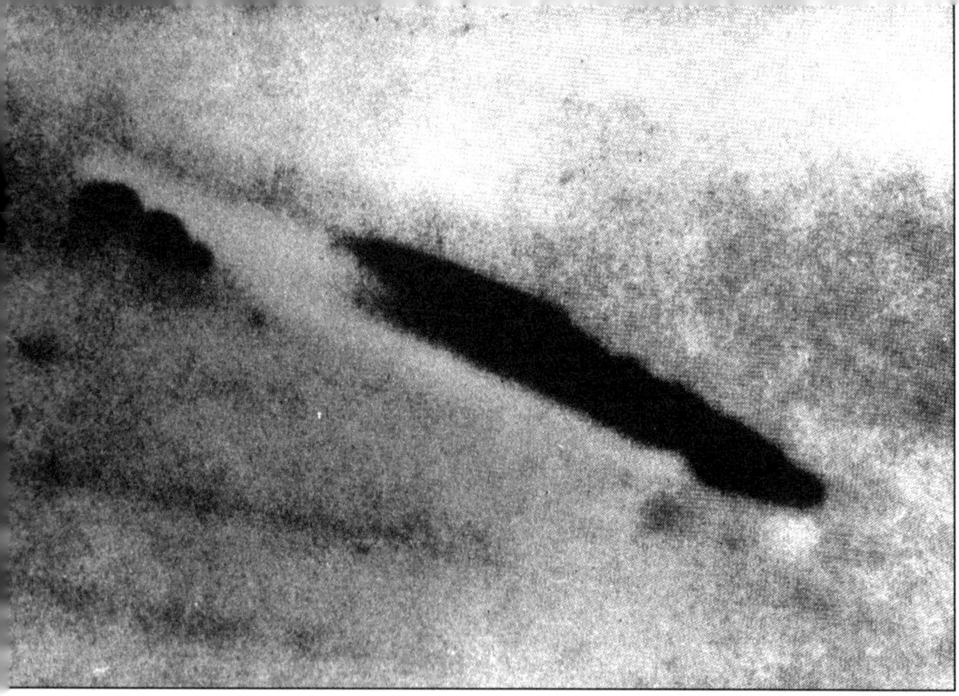

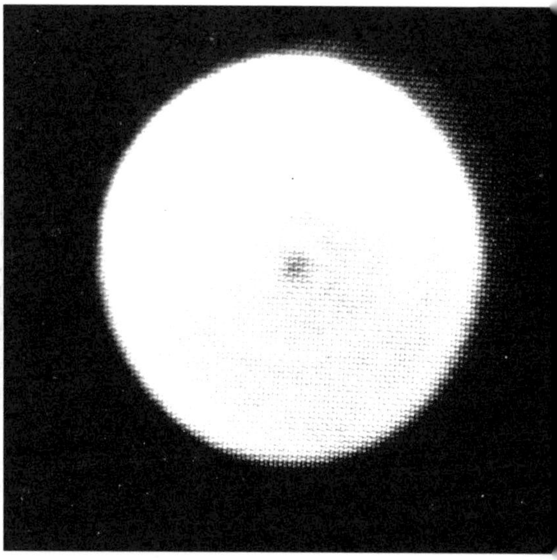

Right: ***A UFO apparently trails a Martin B-57 bomber as it flies near Edwards Air Force Base, California, in September 1957. No one in the B-57 or the accompanying aircraft detected the UFO (enlarged,*** **above*****) at the time; its image emerged only when the film was processed. Sceptics have suggested the image is the result of a flaw in the film.***

Above right: ***A UFO tracked and filmed for minutes on end by a New Zealand TV camera crew flying near the Clarence River in December 1978.***

Ministry commission investigated the site on 18 September, and removed the wrecked upper aerial of Post No 12 for study. Unnamed military sources claimed to have examined the site of the event and seen tapes of the initial series of radar returns.

The description of both these on-screen radar effects and the craft itself suggests all the characteristics of 'stealth' technology – another instance of a UFO suddenly adopting an ultra-modern but little-understood technological disguise. While the 'flash' and the destruction of the radar post could have been caused by a plain missile, it seems unlikely that an American stealth aircraft would have perpetrated such a provocation. And the USAF is the only military force known to have that kind of advanced aircraft in service.

SCORCHED EARTH

The notorious crop circles that plagued British farmers during the 1980s and early 1990s were very soon identified by some enthusiastic devotees of the paranormal as traces of UFO activity. However, the increasing elaborateness of the circles, the emergence of possible scientific explanations and finally the confessions of hoaxers have somewhat reduced the strength of the 'UFO hypothesis'. While hoaxers were certainly not responsible for all the circles, and even the scientists admit their explanation is far from complete, the evidence for UFOs in the usually accepted sense of the term being involved seems remote.

Among the commonest ground effects left by UFOs, however, is evidence of burning.

Over a period of two hours or so during the day of 8 October 1978, various members of the Sturgess family noticed 'something' in a field close to their house (the property is near Jenkins, Missouri) but thought little of it until it rose in the air. Six family members saw the object move away and meet another object; both then vanished, in broad daylight. Inspection of the site where the thing had been resting revealed a 4 ft circle of scorched grass, within which were three smaller circles burnt into the ground. Scientific analysis showed nothing unusual about the samples taken, however.

Samples of earth taken from a site at Medford, Minnesota, after a UFO was seen landing there on 2 November 1975 did, however, reveal some curious qualities. In radiation tests conducted by the Space Technology Laboratory at the University of Kansas, Lawrence, the samples showed ten times the thermo-luminescence of control samples from near the site, but appeared identical under the microscope. Dr Edward Zellner, the university's professor of geology, physics and astronomy, called these variations 'unusual' and 'an anomaly,' but added: 'Like so much of the other data [that] has been obtained on the UFO phenomenon, the results...are inconclusive.'

Below: ***Cameras can lie. This apparent formation of four UFOs was photographed by a US coastguard at the Salem, Massachusetts, Air Station in August 1952. Analysis has shown that the 'lights in the sky' are actually reflections of terrestrial lights on to the camera lens.***

Above: ***One of many UFOs photographed by contactee Daniel Fry in the 1960s. Few experts have taken these pictures at face value since computer analysis has shown that the 'flying saucers' are almost certainly models suspended close to the camera.***

On 30 September 1980, an extraordinary series of effects accompanied the UFO witnessed by 'Mr B', a farmhand and caretaker on a 600 acre property five miles from Rosedale, Victoria, in Australia. At about 1 am, Mr B woke to the sound of the farm's cattle going wild – accompanied by 'a strange screeching whistling'. He got up to investigate. There was no wind, and the moon was out; Mr B saw a domed object about 15 ft high and 25 ft broad with a white top, showing blue and orange lights. For a while it hovered over a concrete water tank about 450 yds from the house, then came to rest on the ground 15 or 20 yds further on.

Mr B clambered on a motorcycle and drove to within 50 ft of the object. There was no effect on his machine, but the whistling from the UFO suddenly rose to deafening heights, there was a huge bang, and the thing lifted off. At the same time, a blast of hot air nearly knocked Mr B over. The UFO dropped some debris and then flew away to the east, holding a height of no more than 100 ft.

FROM WITHIN THE RING OF BURNT GRASS THE FLOWERS HAD DISAPPEARED, BUT STRANGEST OF ALL, 10,000 GALLONS OF WATER HAD BEEN STOLEN.

Right: ***Masato Kohno points to a burn mark left by the UFO he saw land in Kofu City, Japan, on 23 February 1975. The witness also maintained that the concrete pile on the right was broken by the mystery craft.***

Mr B examined the site early next day. He found a ring of blackened grass, flattened in an anti-clockwise direction. Inside the ring was green grass, but flowers that had been growing there had disappeared. In a line to the east outside the ring was a trail of debris – stones, weeds and cow dung. For some days after the sighting Mr B suffered from headaches and nausea, and his watch refused to work normally. Strangest of all, the water tank over which the UFO had paused had been emptied of 10,000 gallons of water.

BIZARRE PHENOMENA

One of the commonest physical reactions to a UFO is the collapse of electrical systems, radios and similar equipment in cars driven by witnesses. This is sometimes, but not always, accompanied by witnesses suffering rashes and nausea after the sighting, a medically recognized reaction to certain kinds of electro-magnetic (EM) radiation. Two cases, more than six years apart and widely separated geographically, show a weird variation on this theme.

Ronald Sullivan was driving on a long, straight stretch of road nine miles east of Bealiba, Victoria, Australia, during the night of 4 April 1966 when his headlight beams suddenly and inexplicably bent part way along their length to the right – as if they had been pieces of pipe. Sullivan screeched to a stop, and was then treated to a brilliant display of coloured lights coming from a field by the road. After that, an object rose up from the field and vanished. Sutherland had his lights checked before reporting the incident to the police; they were in perfect order. When the police investigated the site they found a circular depression about 5 ft across and 5 in at its deepest in the field. Sullivan reported that he 'did not believe in UFOs'.

Six and a half years later, something similar occurred at Taize, in eastern France. At about 1 am on 11 August 1972, a group of about 30 people gathered at the Protestant monastery there, witnessed a 90 ft long UFO hovering against a hillside opposite the building. This then gave a bizarre light display that involved apparently solid beams of light extending slowly to the ground. Four of those present decided to take a closer look, and went across the fields toward it armed with torches. After about 600 yds they came across a dark mass about 20 ft high and shaped like a haystack. When they shone their torches at it, the beams turned upwards at right angles just a foot or so from the object.

Neither case has been satisfactorily explained, although it is perhaps worth noting that the EM effects here occurred on an unusual frequency – that of visible light – rather than on the longer radio wavelengths that more commonly are affected by UFOs. Even this is not much help, since so many of the data on UFOs are concerned precisely with bizarre phenomena involving light.

THE BLACK MASS DEFLECTED THE BEAMS OF THE TORCHES AND REFUSED TO REVEAL ITS DARK SECRETS.

Below: ***An early witness report form used by the British journal* Flying Saucer Review *in the 1950s.***

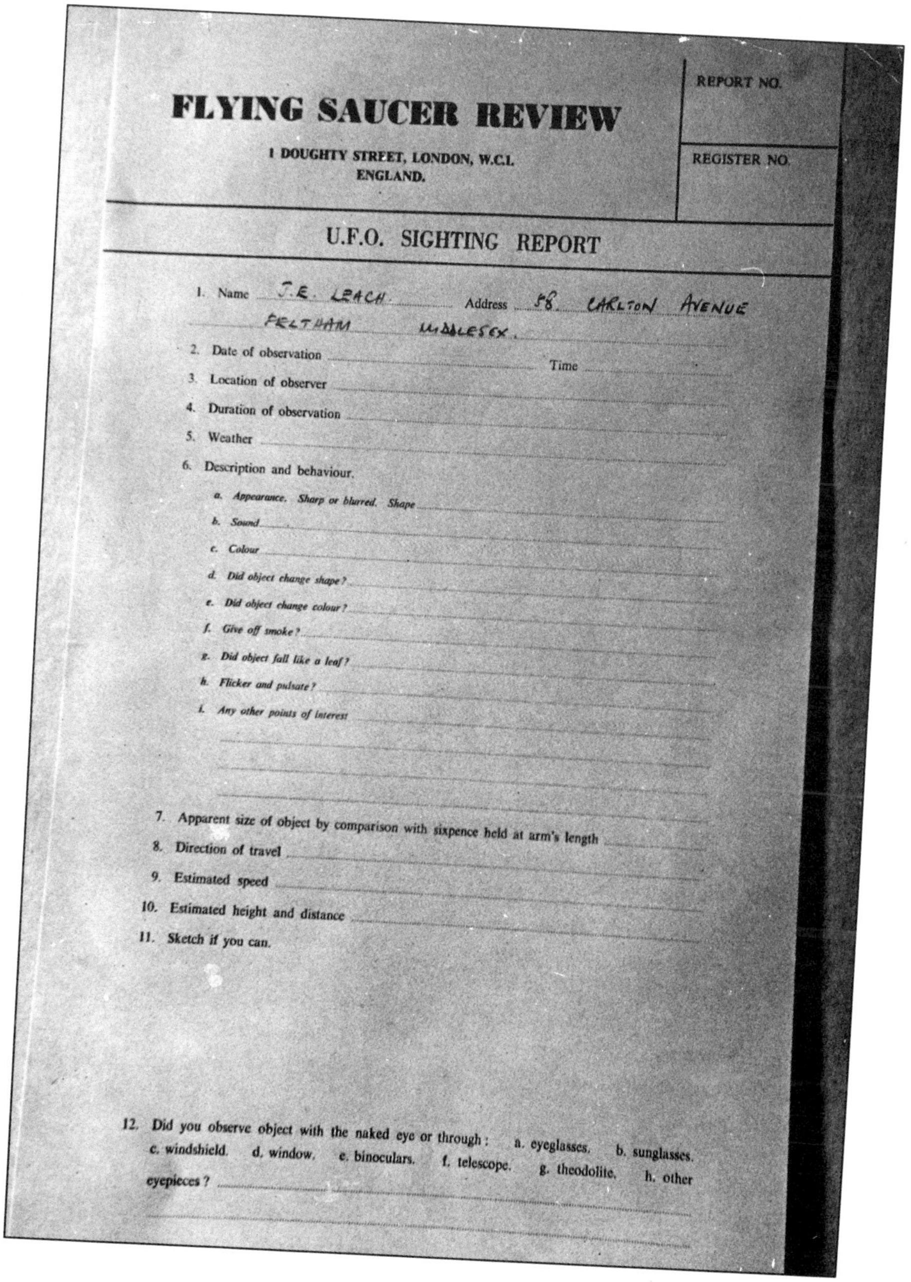
FLYING SAUCER REVIEW
1 DOUGHTY STREET, LONDON, W.C.1.
ENGLAND.

REPORT NO.

REGISTER NO.

U.F.O. SIGHTING REPORT

1. Name J.E. LEACH. Address 58 CARLTON AVENUE FELTHAM MIDDLESEX.
2. Date of observation Time
3. Location of observer
4. Duration of observation
5. Weather
6. Description and behaviour.
   a. Appearance. Sharp or blurred. Shape
   b. Sound
   c. Colour
   d. Did object change shape?
   e. Did object change colour?
   f. Give off smoke?
   g. Did object fall like a leaf?
   h. Flicker and pulsate?
   i. Any other points of interest
7. Apparent size of object by comparison with sixpence held at arm's length
8. Direction of travel
9. Estimated speed
10. Estimated height and distance
11. Sketch if you can.
12. Did you observe object with the naked eye or through: a. eyeglasses, b. sunglasses, c. windshield, d. window, e. binoculars, f. telescope, g. theodolite, h. other eyepieces?

Accidental or deliberately engineered? By a creature of the Earth – or from deep space?

Below: ***Researchers in the 1950s used a chart of basic UFO types to help classify sightings. Note the variety of shapes and configurations – an aspect of UFOs that remains unchanged to this day.***

MARKS OF THE MIND

The disparate forms of the different entities seen around UFOs, the variety of shapes and sizes of the craft themselves (if craft they are), the rarity and ambiguity of the physical evidence: all these suggest that the UFO is not one thing, but several – and possibly many.

How does the UFO phenomenon divide up, given the evidence we have? What *kinds* of UFO are there?

The first essential distinction to make is that in many cases something undoubtedly physical has presented itself to witnesses. But what kind of physical thing is it? There are six possibilities worth serious consideration:

- UFOs are alien craft from planets in outer space.
- UFOs are alien craft from a shy and elusive culture that shares our Earth and perhaps our Solar System.
- UFOs are secret terrestrial craft, probably military in origin, which hide behind a screen of 'flying saucer myths'.
- UFOs are not 'nuts and bolts' craft of any kind, but some kind of biological phenomenon – although some (those without apparent occupants) may possibly be wild creatures, while those with occupants may have been domesticated.
- UFOs are natural phenomena that are related to ball lightning, plasma, and other little-understood manifestations of physics.
- UFOs are intrusions, accidental or deliberately engineered, from other physical dimensions or parallel universes.

As the reported behaviour of UFOs is so varied, it is quite possible that each of these hypotheses is true for a particular set of circumstances – although some of them are more probable than others. But there is no law to say that if UFOs are physical objects, they *have* to be all the same kind of object.

On the other hand they may not be objects at all. Not all UFOs leave physical

traces, and many are seen by only a single witness, even over highly populated areas. So it is not inconceivable that the UFO phenomenon is an entirely psychological – even psychic – one. There are three major hypotheses that attempt to account for UFOs as immaterial phenomena:

- UFOs are hallucinations, triggered by some actual event but confined in reality to the mind of the witness.
- UFOs are indeed hallucinations, but the mental event has been induced by an alien intelligence, either from deep space or from nearer at hand. Both this and the previous suggestion would explain why UFOs present themselves in forms that are appropriate to the particular era in which the witness lives.
- UFOs are material objects – but they are brought into being only by the unconscious psychic working of the witness – or even by the working of the mass unconscious.

Once again it is not outside the bounds of possibility that all three explanations are true, one or another applying to differing circumstances and different sets of evidence.

However, there is another possibility. *All nine of the hypotheses offered here may be correct* – in other words, it may be the case that some UFOs are indeed hallucinations, while some are natural physical and biological phenomena, some are alien craft, others are military in origin, and so on. Just as there is no rule that dictates that all UFOs must be physical objects, so there is no law to say that UFO sightings must be *either* physical *or* psychic events. They may be one or the other; they may on occasion even be a mixture of both, the product of an interaction between physical and psychological states, planes of being, or even dimensions.

Judging from a number of remarks that he made in private, it is likely that it was some such insight that J. Allen Hynek had in mind when he suggested that UFOs should make us 'consider an aspect of reality of which we have been hitherto largely unaware'. The UFO phenomenon is almost unique in exhibiting almost every aspect of the paranormal there is; the physical traces that we have been considering in this chapter may, in fact, be the marks left by the mind – although whether it is the human mind at work here, or the mind of someone or something else, we cannot be certain.

Above: ***Ball lightning, photographed in Austria in summer 1978. Some researchers believe that all alleged UFOs are little-known or poorly understood natural phenomena such as this.***

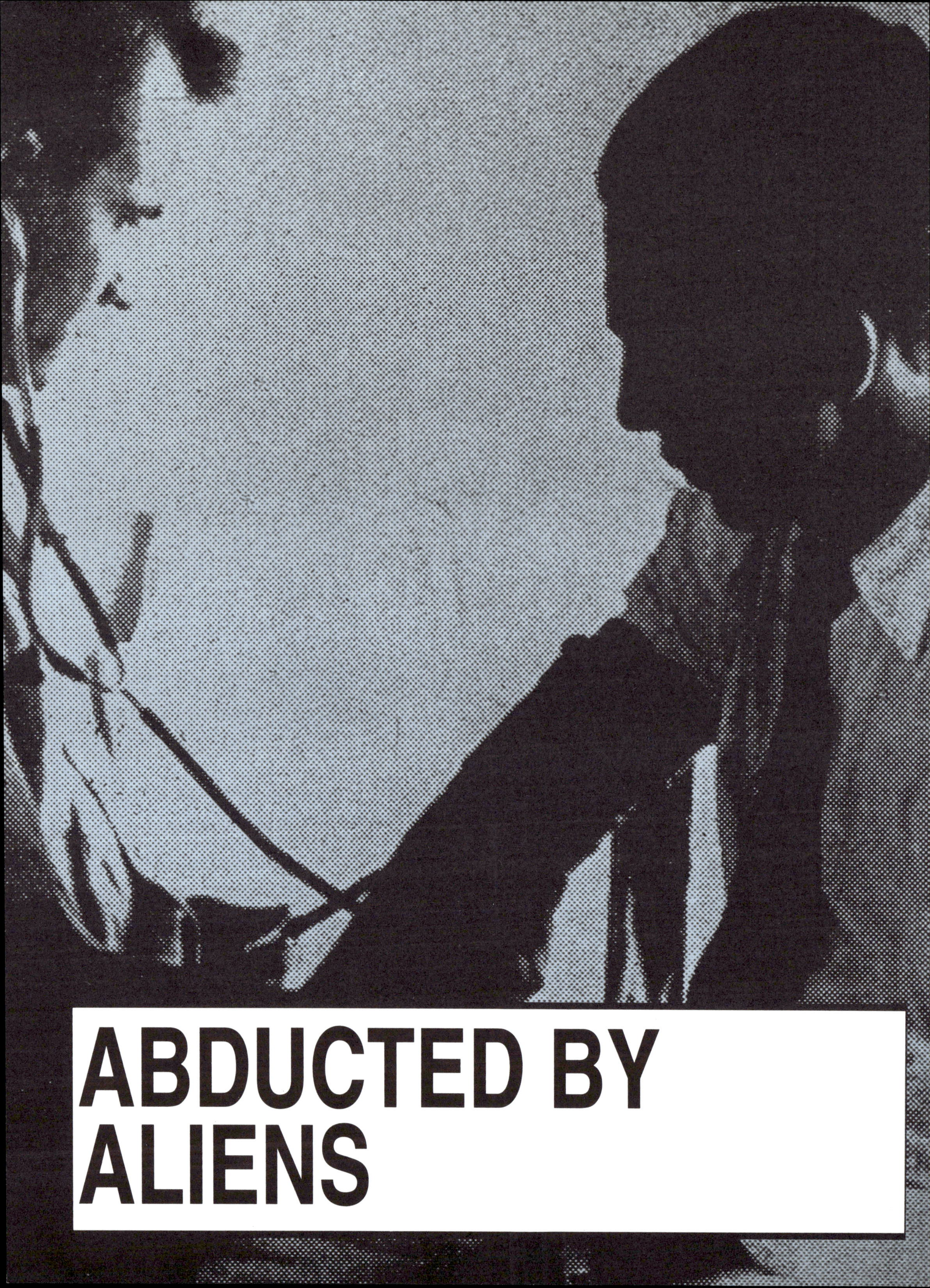

ABDUCTED BY ALIENS

Sensational stories of abduction and grotesque sexual experiments carried out by aliens may be easy to discount, but how do the 'experts' discredit the consistent testimony of a respected sober-suited lawyer?

At the age of 23, Antonio Villas Boas lived a hard but simple life with his parents, his brothers and sisters-in-law on a small farm near the town of São Francisco de Salles, in the Brazilian state of Minas Gerais. With his brothers, Villas Boas worked the farm: while the family had hired help in during the day, Antonio worked at night. On the night of 15–16 October 1957, he was out alone, ploughing the fields by the light of his tractor's headlamps.

He may not have been entirely surprised when, at about 1 am, he saw what he described as a 'large red star' descending out of the sky toward the end of the field he was working. At about 9.30 pm the previous evening, he had been out ploughing with his brother, and the pair had seen a dim red ball of light hovering about 300 ft above the northern end of the field they were working. He had then tried to get close to the light to see what was behind it, but it eluded him, darting from one end of the field to the other.

But this time Villas Boas was alone, and petrified, for as the red light came down to about 150 ft above him, he could see that it was an apparently egg-shaped object. Its brilliant glow drowned out the lights of his tractor as it landed – lowering three shafts as an undercarriage – no more than 50 ft from where he was sitting. The machine had a definite rim, in which were set purple lights. Three spurs were set at the front, lit up with red light. The upper, domed part of the machine was spinning anti-clockwise, and as it slowed to land, it changed colour from red to green.

Antonio tried to escape on his tractor, but the engine died after a few yards. He jumped from the seat and started to struggle across the ploughed field. Then someone grabbed him from behind. He knocked the creature flying, but was grabbed by three others – none higher than his shoulder, and he is only 5 ft 5 in tall – and dragged to the waiting craft. He was taken struggling up a flexible ladder into the machine, and found himself in a small, square, brightly lit room with metallic walls.

He realized that there were five small entities present: two kept a firm hold on him. They were wearing tight-fitting suits of thick, soft, unevenly striped grey material, and large, broad helmets reinforced with bands of metal. Pipes led down from the helmets to their clothes, two

Antonio Villas Boas (opposite, *undergoing medical tests in 1958) had one of the most extraordinary close encounters in the annals of ufology in October 1957. During his brief but astonishing visit on board an alien craft he attempted to steal a piece of equipment as evidence of his experience, but was thwarted. But he was able to recall a sign over one of the doors inside the vehicle* (below) *and reproduce it for investigators.*

going under each armpit and one down their backs. Thick-soled 'shoes' seemed to be integral to their suits, as did thick, unwieldy gloves. All Villas Boas could see of the creatures' features through the helmets were their small, pale blue eyes.

He was then taken into another bright room, this time oval-shaped. Here, the aliens first attempted a conversation with their captive. Villas Boas later recalled that the sounds they made 'were so totally different from anything I had heard...They were slow barks and yelps, neither very clear nor very hoarse, some longer, some shorter, at times containing several different sounds all at once...But they were simply sounds, animal barks...I still shudder when I think of those sounds. I can't reproduce them – my voice just isn't made for that.'

Failing to communicate in words, the five diminutive aliens then proceeded to strip the protesting farmer of his clothes. One of the beings rubbed a wet sponge-like thing over his skin, and then he was led through still another door. This had an inscription over it in red 'letters', which he was able to reproduce later for investigators. (At first glance, this looks very like hastily scribbled Arabic, but it seems to relate to no known terrestrial alphabet.) In this chamber, sparsely furnished with a few chairs and a couch, the aliens produced 'a sort of chalice', which they used to take a blood sample. Then Villas Boas was left alone – only to find a weird odour filling the room, which soon had him rushing to a corner of the room to be sick. After that he began to calm down. But then came the most bizarre part of his experience aboard the alien ship.

SEXUAL ENCOUNTERS

He had been standing there naked for perhaps half an hour when the door to the

Below: ***A UFO approaches a witness and disgorges three aliens during a close encounter near Pirassununga, São Paulo, Brazil, in September 1976. When there is dialogue between aliens and witnesses, the encounter is classified as of the 'fourth kind'. Close encounters of the fifth kind are full-scale abductions.***

room opened – to reveal a woman whose body was 'more beautiful than any I have ever seen before'. This was something Antonio could hardly help noticing, for she was entirely nude.

The woman stood shoulder-high to him. Her hair was parted in the middle, and reached halfway down her neck before it curled inward. It was smooth, fair, almost white, except for her armpits and pubic hair, which was bright red. She had a pointed chin, straight nose, high cheekbones, and large blue eyes. Her arms were freckled. Her body, said Villas Boas, was 'slim, and her breasts stood up high and well separated. Her waistline was thin, her belly flat, her hips well developed, and her thighs were large.' What happened next was perhaps inevitable, and best told in Antonio Villas Boas's own words:

'The woman came toward me in silence, looking at me all the while as if she wanted something from me, and suddenly she hugged me and began to rub her head against my face from side to side. At the same time I also felt her body glued to mine and it also was moving.'

Villas Boas wondered if the liquid the aliens had spread on him had been some kind of stimulant, but he, at least, needed none:

'We ended up on the couch, where we lay together for the first time. It was a normal act and she reacted as any other woman would. Then we had some petting, followed by another act, but by now she had begun to deny herself to me, to end the matter.'

At that, Antonio too lost interest – and became angry, as it dawned on him that 'all they wanted [was] a good stallion to improve their stock...but [I] decided not to attach any importance to the fact, for

Above: ***UFO photographed by contactee Elizabeth Klarer in South Africa in the 1950s. Klarer was not abducted by ufonauts – she went willingly and, she claimed, lived with one on his home planet, where she gave birth to their child.***

THE ALIENS WERE AFTER A GOOD 'STALLION' TO IMPROVE THEIR STOCK – AND THE BEAUTIFUL BLONDE MADE IT EASY TO OBLIGE.

anyhow I had spent a few agreeable moments with the woman'. His impression that he was being used in a quite calculating fashion may have been reinforced by the fact that the woman never kissed him, although she did bite him gently on the chin.

Shortly after this (it seems not to have occurred to Villas Boas that his activities were possibly being monitored) the woman was called away. Before she left, she pointed to her stomach, and then at the sky, which he interpreted as meaning that sooner or later she, and the other aliens, would return to take him away. Brazilian investigators persuaded him, however, that she had simply meant that she would bear their child on her home planet. After this, Antonio Villas Boas was given back his clothes and taken on a guided tour of the alien craft, during which he tried, and failed, to purloin an instrument as a keepsake. Then he was carried back down the ladder to the ground, from where he saw the UFO take off, listing slightly to one side and then disappearing into the sky like a bullet. He had been aboard the craft for 4 hours, 15 minutes.

Charles Hickson (above) *and his colleague Calvin Parker claimed that they were abducted by aliens in Pascagoula, Mississippi, in October 1973. The sketch* (right) *shows Hickson's own impression of one of the entities aboard the craft.*

THE TERRIFIED ABDUCTEES WERE OFTEN STRIPPED AND SUBJECTED TO A PAINFUL MEDICAL EXAMINATION.

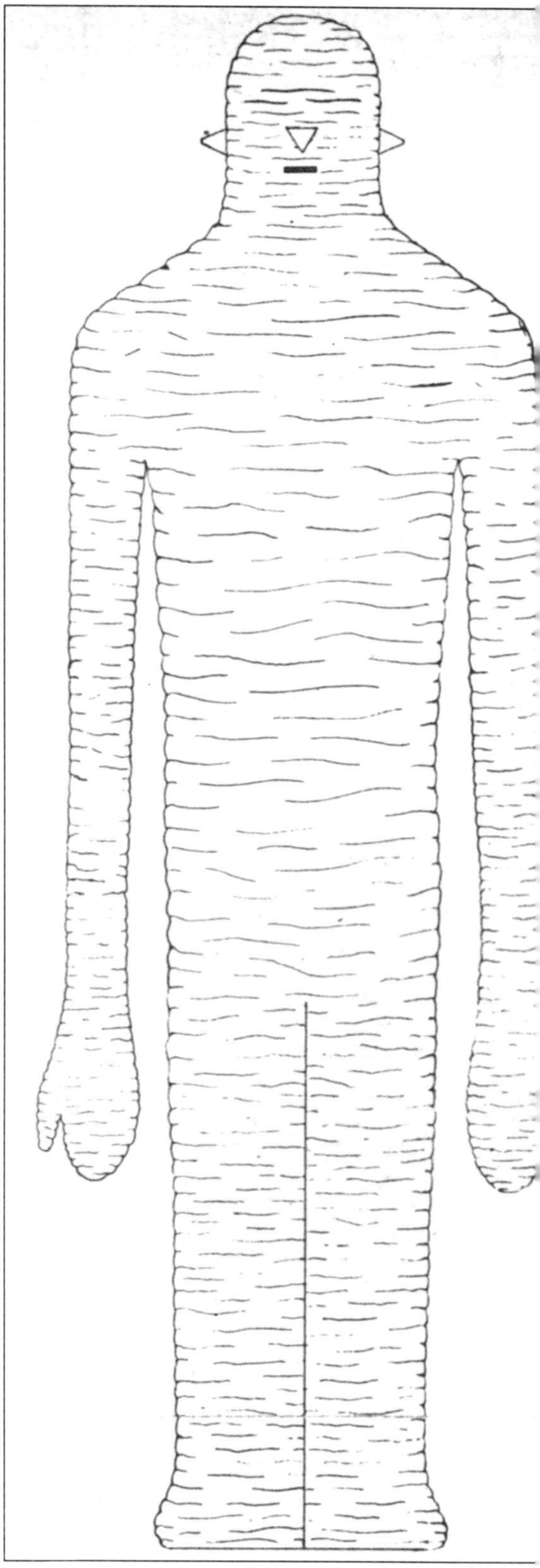

The Villas Boas case boggled the UFO investigators who heard about it so much that it was not until 12 years after these events that the witness's name was published. While the case became a classic in ufology, little was heard about Villas Boas himself. But in 1978 he surfaced again on a TV programme in Brazil – no longer a simple peasant farmer, but Dr Antonio Villas Boas, a sober lawyer with a practice in a small town near the nation's capital, Brasilia, happily married and with four children. The only item of his testimony that he changed was minor: the woman had taken a sperm sample from him during their second act of intercourse.

To the determined sceptic, the Villas Boas case has always been the fantasy of a simple Brazilian rustic. Yet the person who experienced what he did in October 1957, and the man who had gained academic distinction and a respected place in his community 21 years later were essentially one and the same. Intelligent, articulate, educated and determined, Dr Villas Boas was revealed as a person who cannot be dismissed any more as a mere 'peasant' – which is to say, ignorant, superstitious, and clod-hopping. And he did not change his mind, or contradict himself, when questioned 21 years later about his abduction.

Perhaps most important, his first account of that bizarre, frightening, yet exciting night was given straight from his conscious memory, and less than four months afterward. Unlike many who have claimed to recall – sometimes more than 20 years after the alleged events – being abducted by aliens and having sometimes grotesque sexual experiences while in their custody, Antonio Villas Boas did not need to be hypnotized to be able to give the most detailed account of what happened to him.

THE 'MISSING TIME'

The 'AVB' case, as it was known among ufologists, was long regarded as almost unique in the annals of abductions in that it involved a sexual encounter – although still more astounding claims were published in German in 1977, by South African Elizabeth Klarer. She maintained that between 1954 and 1963 she had numerous meetings with the two-man crew of a craft from the planet Meton, in the solar system of Proxima Centauri, the nearest star to the Sun, 4.3 light-years away. One of the aliens, the astrophysicist Akon, became the father of her child, and Klarer says she spent four months on Meton before her son was born, after which she was obliged to return to Earth while he remained on Meton with his father. Few ufologists took Klarer's claims seriously – as so often with contactees who allege they have visited known star systems, the laws of celestial mechanics spoil her story. Proxima Centauri is part of the triple-star system of Alpha Centauri, and as such is highly unlikely to have any planets. And even if it did, the star is a red dwarf – too small and too feeble to support life of any kind.

The typical pattern of abductee accounts did not, until the 1980s, involve any specifically sexual component at all. The classic scenario is reflected in the well-known accounts given by Betty and Barney Hill (abducted in New Hampshire in 1961), Betty Andreasson (in Massachusetts, 1967), Calvin Parker and Charlie Hickson (in Mississippi, 1973), David Stephens (in Maine, 1975), Whitley Strieber (in New York State, 1985) and others.

The events reported by these witnesses followed this basic pattern: first came a UFO sighting, sometimes involving electro-magnetic effects or other physical effects on the witnesses' vehicles. A key factor in the vast majority of such cases

Above: ***Betty Andreasson, who was abducted by aliens in Massachusetts in 1967 and given a bizarre 'pregnancy test' during her captivity.***

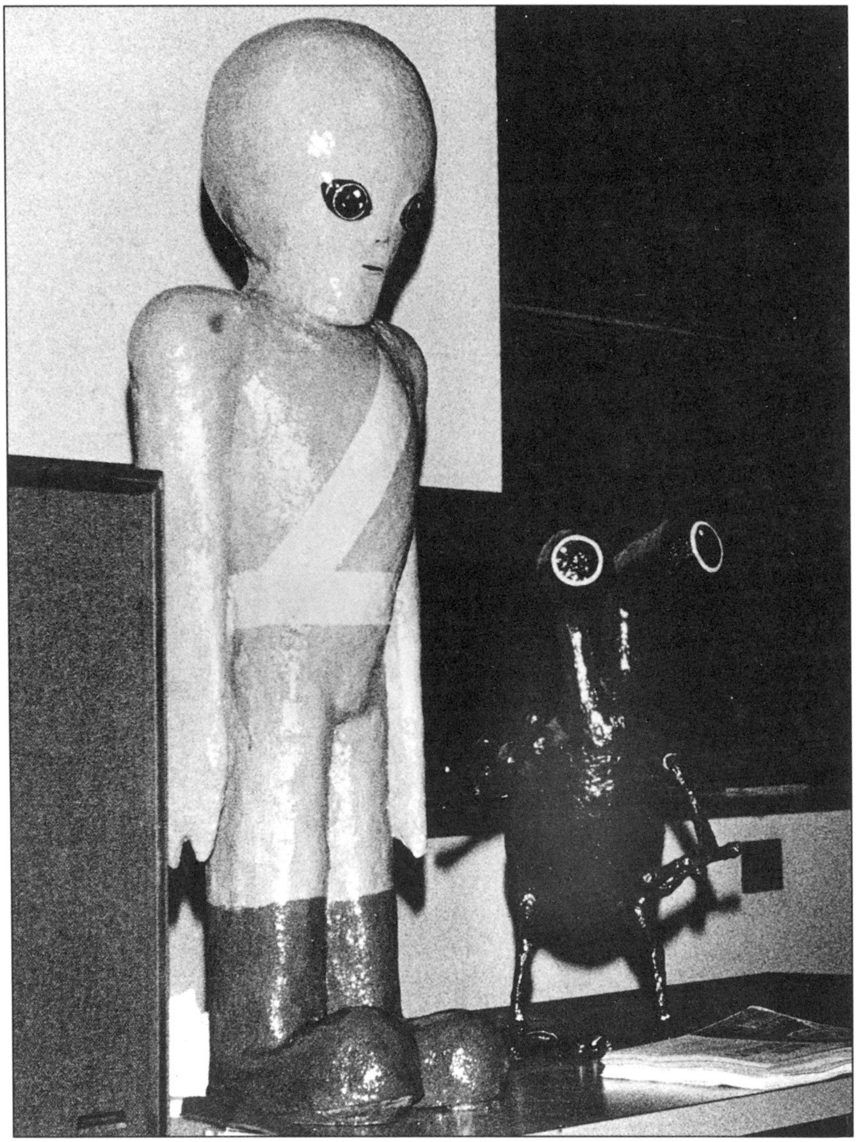

aliens and the exterior of their ships often differ wildly from case to case.

Interiors of alien craft are, according to these witnesses, usually brightly lit, clinically clean, often shiny, with white or metallic appurtenances. The reason for this soon becomes clear, for the next stage in the abduction is a medical examination of some kind – usually a painful one.

Betty Hill and Betty Andreasson independently reported that they were examined with a machine from which needle-like wires protruded. Charles Hickson said his body was 'scanned' by a floating instrument resembling a large eye. Betty Hill and Betty Andreasson also said that needles were inserted into their navels for a 'pregnancy test'. Betty Hill had skin scrapings, samples of ear wax, hair and clippings from her fingernails taken from her. David Stephens had two blood samples taken, and was undressed and examined from head to toe with 'a box-like device'. Whitley Strieber maintained that 'an enormous and extremely ugly object', triangular in structure and with a tangle of wires at one end, was inserted into his rectum.

After this, the witnesses report, they are either allowed to dress and leave the ship – some are 'transferred' directly from the craft or 'floated' back to where the aliens first took them captive – or, occasionally,

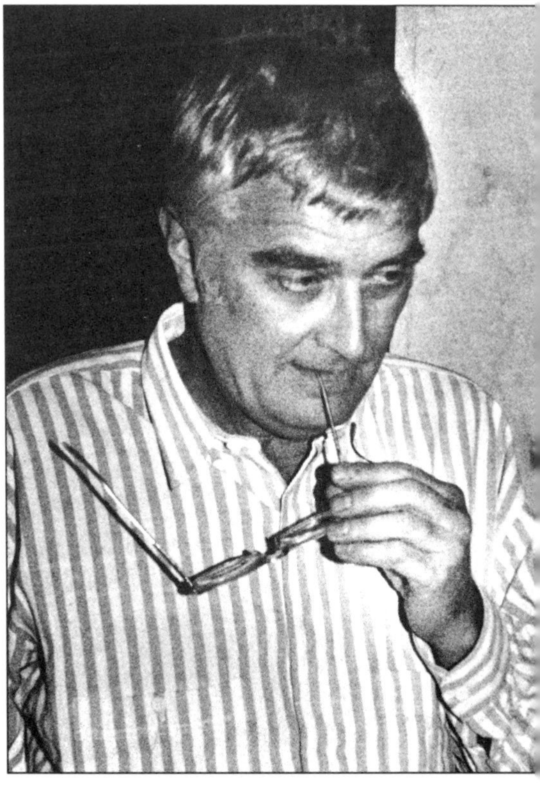

Above: ***A model of 'Quazgaa', one of the alien entities that took part in the abduction and medical examination of Betty Andreasson.***

Right: ***Artist Budd Hopkins, who believes that visiting aliens are performing a programme of genetic manipulation on the human race.***

emerges after the UFO has departed: the events of what seem like a few minutes' duration turn out to have taken an hour or more. The witnesses duly report their sighting to the police, local military authorities or the sheriff's office. Of their own accord, or encouraged by their family or members of a UFO investigation organization, witnesses then undergo hypnosis in an attempt to bring out the buried memory of what transpired in the crucial 'missing time' during their UFO encounter.

However, a handful of abductees do have clear memories of this part of their experience and need no such prompting or psychological dredging. But their descriptions of what happened to them in this segment of 'missing time' closely match the reports of hypnotized subjects even though the physical appearance of the given a guided tour around the ship first. Once the victims have been returned to their starting point, the UFO leaves at high speed.

GENETIC SAMPLING

The reality, or otherwise, of UFO abductions became a major controversy among ufologists in the 1980s, and excited massive public attention as well. Budd Hopkins, a New York artist who as a result of his own UFO sighting became fascinated by abduction stories, used hypnotic techniques to uncover numerous witnesses' hidden memories of such experiences, and the bestselling book (later made into a film) *Communion* by novelist Whitley Strieber, in which he recounted his own gruesome and humiliating experiences as an abductee, was based on events recalled under hypnosis.

Undoubtedly, Hopkins's book received huge attention in the media because of the new element he had discovered in the cases he had investigated: and that was a constant sexual slant to the stories. Men reported having devices applied to them that relieved them of their sperm. Still greater number of women, notably one named Kathie Davis, told stories under hypnosis that suggested to Hopkins that aliens were conducting a deliberate and sustained programme of genetic sampling and possibly even manipulation among the human race, who were mostly unaware of what was being done to it.

According to Hopkins, hypnosis revealed that aliens first visited Kathie Davis when she was a child, and had implanted a device in her head so that they could keep track of her. (She and other members of her family had similar, mysterious scars on their legs, which Hopkins attributed to cell-sampling by the aliens, noting that other alleged abductees bore similar marks.) As a teenager, Kathie became pregnant, but the pregnancy ended suddenly and mysteriously. Hypnosis revealed that before her pregnancy, aliens had visited Kathie, performed an 'uncomfortable' and intimate procedure, and departed. Some months later they returned and removed her feotus. Years later, after she had married and had two children, the aliens returned again and briefly presented her with a little girl who 'looked like an elf or an...angel'. This was, apparently, her extra-terrestrially induced daughter. Kathie Davis was not the only woman who, according to Hopkins's research, had been impregnated by ufonauts.

Above: ***Novelist Whitley Strieber, who built a best-selling book,*** **Communion,** ***around his alleged abduction by ufonauts in 1985. Since then, he has hinted that the account is a fantasy.***

A FLAWED TOOL

Many serious ufologists – across the whole spectrum of the subject, from ardent 'believers' to those who border on scepticism – have had serious doubts about the validity of abduction accounts ever since George Adamski claimed to have met a Venusian in the California desert.

If, however – as is at least possible – the 'UFO experience' is a peculiar blend of material and psychic realities, there may be a kernel of truth in many abduction reports – though it may be truth of a very strange kind. But there is a vast difference between the account of a man like Dr Antonio Villas Boas and the stories that Budd Hopkins has

Psychologist Carl Gustav Jung **(above)** *believed that a number of archetypal figures – from wise old men to monstrous semi-human creatures – lie buried in everyone's unconscious, emerging in the dreams of individuals and the myths and legends of whole societies. Jung considered UFOs to be a symbol of humanity's state of mind, projected on to the environment. Jung would no doubt have been fascinated had he lived long enough to learn that UFO occupants seem to follow the same patterns of appearance and behaviour as the archetypal figures that he identified in the collective unconscious.*

put into mass circulation – and the key to that difference is the use of hypnosis.

Despite its many virtues in other contexts, hypnosis is notoriously unreliable as a tool for probing the memory, unless the hypnotist is scrupulously careful in the style and content of the questioning. One particular problem is that a false memory, unconsciously and even innocently suggested to the subject by the hypnotist through a leading question, will become part of ordinary conscious memory – and its impression, its apparent reality, will grow stronger the more the subject returns to it under hypnosis.

There is a powerful feeling among ufologists that Hopkins's conclusions from his hypnosis of apparent abductees are severely flawed. Critics say that he is too biased in his own beliefs to make a good examiner. Hopkins is not trained as either a hypnotist or a psychologist, and critics say he asks blatantly leading questions – letting the subject know the kind of answer that would please him most – and that he breaks all the other rules, too, that expert hypnotists observe.

Most damning of all to his case that for decades aliens have been performing genetic experiments on human subjects, a number of Hopkins's star witnesses have publicly repudiated the idea that they have been abducted. In 1987, the central character in his book *Intruders*, Kathie Davis, said bluntly at the US Mutual UFO Network's symposium in Washington DC: 'I can live with it because I don't believe it. I *really* don't. There's got to be something else' – in other words, another explanation.

Whitley Strieber, who in 1987 received $1 million in advance royalties for his best-selling book *Communion*, admitted in 1991 that there might be some quite different explanation for his experience besides an 'alien abduction'. Attentive readers of the book itself might have guessed as much, for in it Strieber recounts how he used to tell a number of dramatic stories about himself as truth but now candidly admits they were fantasies.

PUZZLING RESULTS

Still more serious is the discovery that under hypnosis, even people who have no knowledge or interest in UFOs will create essentially the same details of an abduction story as are reported by people who believe that they have actually been abducted.

This astonishing and potentially devastating piece of research was conducted in 1977 by Prof. Alvin Lawson, Dr W.C. McCall and ufologist John DeHerrerra at Anaheim Memorial Hospital, near Los Angeles. The experiment was inspired by the puzzling results of an investigation that DeHerrerra had conducted into a UFO sighting. In the hope of gaining further details of the event, the witness, Brian Scott, had agreed to be hypnotized and 'regressed' (that is, taken back in time) to the time of his encounter. In his hypnotic trance he had described being abducted by aliens. But in his normal waking state, Scott vehemently insisted that no such abduction had taken place.

Lawson and his colleagues recruited 16 volunteers who, in Lawson's words, 'knew little and cared less' about UFOs. They were given the bare bones of a typical abduction story: seeing a UFO land, being taken aboard and seeing the inside of the spacecraft, and being 'examined' by the aliens. The subjects of the experiment were simply asked, at each stage, what they saw or felt happening. And in detail after

Left: ***One of the frightening goblin-like creatures that besieged the Sutton farm at Kelly, Hopkinsville, Kentucky, in 1955, makes a determined attack on one of the family members. The creatures were archetypal fiends or demons such as are found in the folklore of every culture. Was the Suttons' experience proof that such beings really exist – or did something else call up these terrifying images from their subconscious minds, perhaps as a disguise for its own purposes?***

elaborate detail, the volunteers poured out images and experiences that were uncannily similar to those described by 'real' UFO abductees.

Lawson also noted that the alien figures described by both genuine claimants and his innocent creators of fictional abductions fitted with basic archetypes that the pioneering psychologist C.G. Jung suggested were part of everyone's unconscious imagery. It would be easy enough to conclude from this that people claiming to have been abducted by UFOs were simply calling on imagery that is buried deep in everyone's unconscious mind. But, interestingly, Lawson did no such thing. In answer to his own question, 'Do these similarities prove that close encounter cases are illusory?', Lawson cited four reasons why abduction reports might still be genuine.

First, he pointed out, many abductions and close encounter reports involve multiple witnesses; that they all would

WHEN THE RESPECTABLE MIDDLE-AGED WOMAN CAME ROUND SHE WAS TIED NAKED TO A METALLIC TABLE INSIDE THE SPACECRAFT. HER ORDEAL WAS ONLY JUST BEGINNING.

have *identical* hallucinations seems highly unlikely. Second, the physical scars that many abductees can show to be a result of their experiences 'suggest that *something* happened'. Third, close encounter witnesses recognize how unlikely the events are that unfold during their experience, yet are convinced of their reality. Fourth, psychologists can identify the 'trigger' that sets most hallucinations running in the human mind, but there is no consistent factor in abduction or encounter cases that lets investigators pinpoint an unmistakably imaginary experience.

Lawson's experiment has been cited time and again by sceptics who claim that it disposes of all abduction claims. But Lawson himself was not so convinced. 'I myself feel certain,' he wrote, 'that accounts given by witnesses reflect what their senses have reported – that is, they do actually perceive humanoids...and so on. But if [the entities they perceive are] already in the collective unconscious, they are already...in the mind of the witness before his close encounter.' The real mystery, Lawson suggested, was not what the witness saw but what stimulated those archetypal images to arise from the witness's unconscious in the first place. Neither he nor his experiment, he admitted, could answer that question.

A BRUTAL ORDEAL

Even if one rejects Budd Hopkins's belief that a secret alien programme of genetic sampling is under way in our midst, a genuine mystery remains – indeed more than just one mystery. One riddle is posed by that handful of abduction cases that have been reported by sober and upright citizens without recourse to hypnosis.

Antonio Villas Boas is not alone in this category. At about 11 pm on 16 October 1973, a 43-year-old woman (who, understandably, insisted on anonymity) was driving along a road near Langford Budville, Somerset, when the electrical system of her car failed. She climbed out to investigate, felt something touch her, and turned to see a 6 ft tall robot-like figure. She fainted on the spot. When she came round, a domed vehicle some 20 ft long and perhaps 40 ft high had appeared next to her. Again she fainted, and came round to

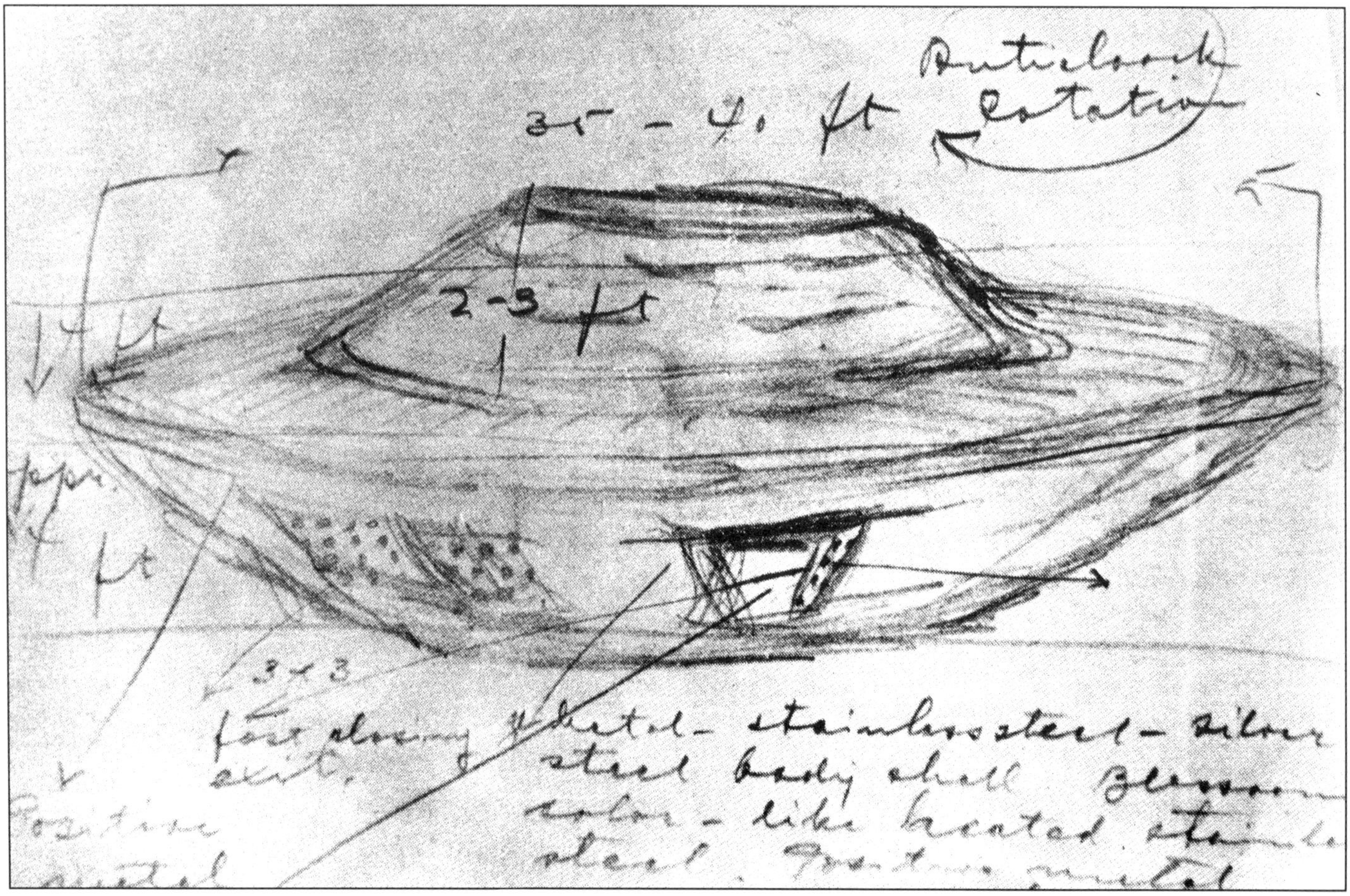

Below: ***Sketch by witness Steve Michalak of a huge metallic UFO, some 35–40 ft in diameter, which he approached and touched in a location near Falcon Lake, Manitoba, Canada, on 20 May 1967. Sightings like this suggest that some, if not all, UFOs are indeed material, 'nuts-and-bolts' craft, although their origins and purposes remain obscure.***

find herself tied naked to a metallic table in a room with glowing walls, inside the craft. When three humanoids – also about 6 ft tall – had finished examining her, two left the room. The third then raped her, and she fainted once more. She came to finally to find herself back in her car – which was now in perfect working order. By now it was 2 am.

But not all conscious abductions have a lurid sexual element. Brazilian military policeman Jose Antonio was on a fishing trip at a lake north of Belo Horizonte, Minas Gerais, one Sunday afternoon in May 1969, when he was paralysed by a burst of light and borne off to an upright, cylindrical craft by two 4 ft tall creatures in masks. Once inside, he was tied up and given a helmet to wear. The machine then took off and after an 'interminable' period, landed. Jose Antonio was next blindfolded and taken to a brilliantly lit room, in which he saw the bodies of four other humans, one of them a Negro, to be interrogated in front of about 15 of the tiny creatures. They removed samples of his fishing gear, and used drawings and sign language to suggest that he be 'their guide among men'. When he refused, he was blindfolded again and returned to Earth. Once on the ground he collapsed, and woke to find himself near Vitoria, in the state of Espirito Santo, 200 miles from where he had been fishing. He subsequently discovered that four and a half days had elapsed between his initial abduction and his return.

If abduction experiences were purely hallucinatory, a pattern would emerge within them, just as patterns are clear enough in states of neurosis and madness. The fact that Budd Hopkins perceives patterns in the abduction cases he has investigated is, in fact, almost as good as a danger sign. The genuine UFO case often signals itself by the way it only partly conforms to a pattern, and has only some aspects in common with previous cases of its kind.

Taken together, what the most genuine-sounding accounts of abduction by aliens most resemble, in fact, is not a pattern of deliberate and calculated intrusions by beings from elsewhere, but a series of bizarre accidents as they might appear to some innocent victims, only partly aware of the full circumstances in which they have been caught up. If there is anything to the notion that UFOs are not extraterrestrial craft from within our own Universe, but exist in parallel with it, this image may prove highly fruitful in both comprehending, and coming to terms with, the entire perplexing enigma.

And not the least important of the answers to these mysteries lies hidden in the human mind, its nature, and its abilities.

THE GRUESOME AND HUMILIATING EXPERIENCES MIGHT BE A COVER-UP FOR A SUSTAINED PROGRAMME OF GENETIC SAMPLING OF THE HUMAN RACE.

Below: ***A mystery flying vehicle beams light into water in Pennsylvania in 1961.***

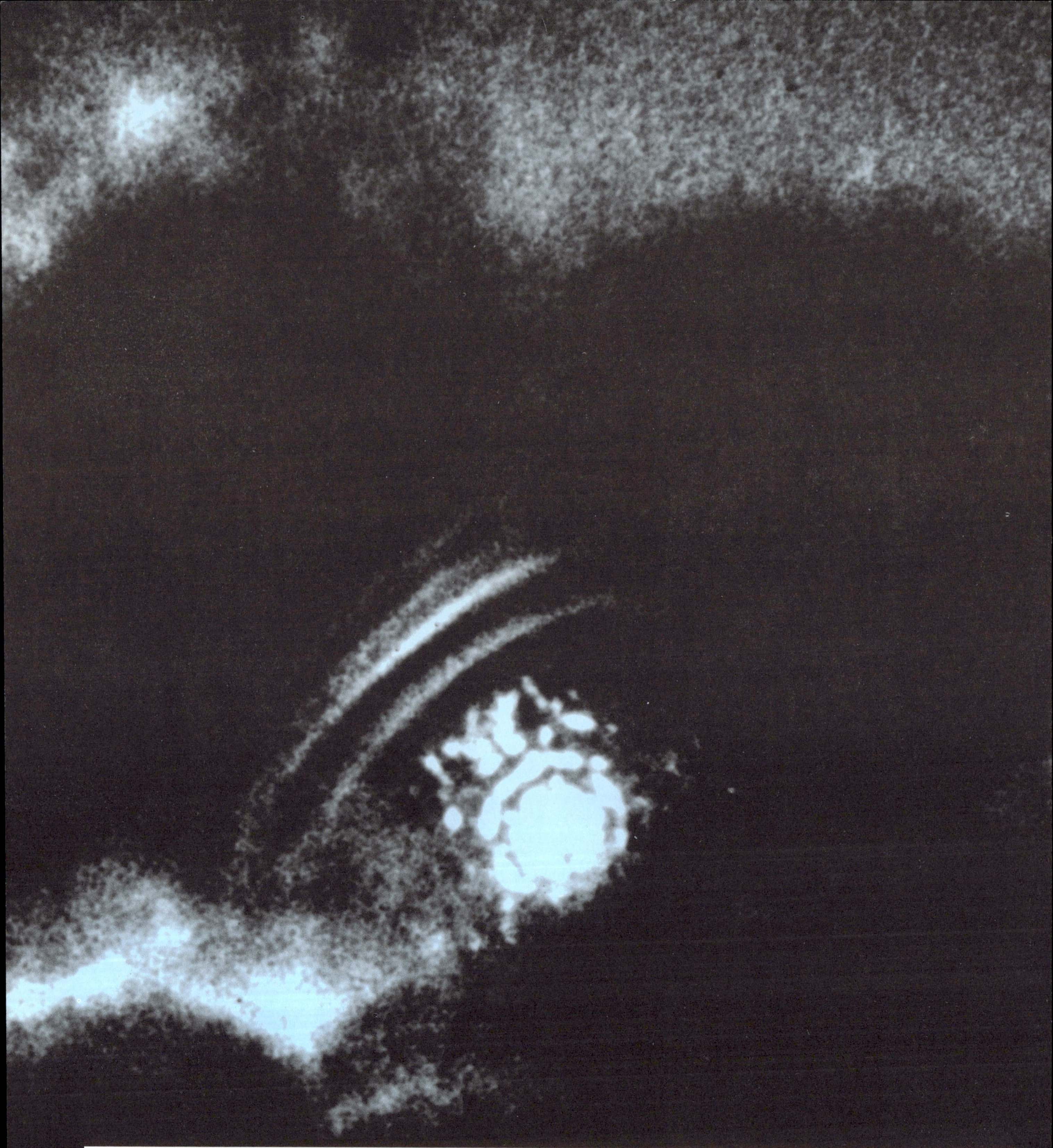

VISITS FROM THE GODS

For centuries individuals have accepted the possibility of alternative realities and other worlds. As humanity rushes headlong to its fate, many wonder about the nature of the beings that may control these realities.

Most people in the West have grown up with some knowledge of a reality that is quite different from that of the everyday world. Some believe in it without question; and while others would deny its existence altogether, the majority probably fall into a grey area of more or less nervous uncertainty. But everyone has an opinion about it, however vague. That other reality is, of course, the religious dimension, which encompasses the notion of God as all-seeing and all-powerful, includes the possibility of an evil power opposed to God, and involves images and traditions concerning the survival of the soul after death.

Whether or not each of us continues to exist in some conscious form when the body dies has little bearing on the problems thrown up by UFOs, but it is absolutely relevant that most people have no hardship in accepting the possibility that another order of reality beside our own may exist – and some people are absolutely convinced of it. (Convinced and committed atheists, on the other hand, are surprisingly hard to find.) This other reality is, besides, by definition beyond our comprehension. Moses hid his face in the presence of God, whose 'explanation' of Himself as I AM THAT I AM can be understood only intuitively, not rationally.

Many people feel similarly awed when confronted by the utterances of the secret priests of our own epoch, scientists and mathematicians. Physicists blithely tell us that certain sub-atomic particles may be seen travelling backwards in time, and that time itself may be stretched, shrunk, or bent. Indeed built into Einstein's theories of relativity is the concept of not a single universe – the one that visibly fills the night sky – but an infinite multiplicity of universes.

Such concepts are extraordinary, but they are grounded in extremely rigorous mathematical proofs. The immemorial claims of religions the world over that there is at least another plane of existence beyond the reach of our immediate senses has thus, in this century, been paralleled by the discoveries of science – although these are no more than parallel ideas: not even the most religious scientist would maintain that he or she has found the source of the Creator.

There are people, however, who would say that the mysteries of religion, of good versus evil, the ultimate fate of humankind,

Above: ***The age-old battle between the forces of good and evil. In this illustration from a 13th-century manuscript, Satan attempts to seize a magician with whom he has made a pact, while a lay brother defends the wizard. Some ufologists believe that UFOs are part of this eternal struggle between the powers of light and the powers of darkness.***

Opposite: ***A UFO photographed over Cheshire, England, by a bank employee in 1987.***

Left: ***Albert Einstein, whose theories of relativity show mathematically that other universes may exist in parallel to the one we inhabit.***

THE SENSE OF HUMOUR DISPLAYED BY SOME UFONAUTS IS OF THE VERY CRUELLEST KIND.

and the mysteries of UFO phenomena, are closely related. To an impartial observer, it may seem that such ideas result from a confusion between the scientific concept of other distinct but equal planes of being, and the religious apprehension of an absolute reality that underpins, justifies and verifies our life on Earth. It would also appear that if genuine UFO entities are really communicating messages of cosmic import, the ufonauts have a singularly cruel sense of humour. These suspicions may seem more reasonable after a survey of what various religious cults have made of the UFO phenomenon.

TELEPATHIC MESSAGES

The longest-lived UFO organization to recognize the religious significance of flying saucers is undoubtedly the Aetherius Society. The society was founded by Western Master of Yoga Sir George King in 1955 following an alleged instruction proclaiming 'Prepare yourself! You are to become the voice of Interplanetary Parliament!'

Sir George King then set up the Aetherius Society in response to growing interest in his messages from a being from Venus called Aetherius. The information that he allegedly received telepathically was, according to the Aetherius Society, relayed over millions of miles of etheric space for the benefit of mankind.

The Aetherius Society believes there is a strong link between man's nuclear activity and the presence of flying saucers. It is claimed that the occupants of these UFOs are concerned that a nuclear disaster on Earth could affect the Solar System too. Therefore, the Aetherius Society considers that part of the role of these aliens is to act as 'guardians' who impart information to mankind which would help avert such a catastrophe.

One of the major missions of the Aetherius Society is to charge 'prayer batteries' designed by Sir George King. In collaboration with various 'space agencies' the prayer energy, often amounting to 2500 'prayer hours', is frequently discharged to areas of the world which are, according to the Aetherius Society, in desperate need of spiritual energy. Pilgrimages are often made to charge these batteries from the tops of holy mountains in various parts of the world, where the adherents form a circle and recite mantras. The society says that often as a result of these efforts, extraterrestrials then add their own energy.

PROPHECIES OF DOOM

Few UFO religious cults have lasted as long as the Aetherius Society. More than one has come to an abrupt end through making grandiose prophecies about future events

Right: ***At 2 pm on 4 February 1990, schoolboy Dima Girenko took this photograph of a UFO in the Achtyrka District of the Ukraine. The Moscow Aviation Institute declared that it was no hoax.***

that then fail to come to pass. One such was Human Individual Metamorphosis (HIM), founded in the mid-1970s by a couple known variously as The Two, Him and Her, Bo and Peep and, to previous acquaintances (who included their former fellow inmates within the Texas penitentiary system, and others at the mental hospital where they met, he as patient and she as nurse), as Marshall Herff Applewhite and Bonnie Lu Nettles. Seized by a sense of destiny, the pair turned up unannounced in small communities around the southern and western states to divulge their message, which Applewhite had received through mediumistic contact with a 19th-century monk.

This was in essence that 'the level above human' was a physical place, and could be reached by UFO. This would happen only when Bo and Peep – who said they were themselves aliens, millions of years old, in human form – had first been assassinated, and left dead in the street for three and a half days: they would then return to life and at this point the UFO would arrive and bear them away. Others could join The Two on the trip to salvation, on condition that they renounced all private possessions and family ties. Astonishingly enough, The Two soon gathered about 1000 disciples.

Unfortunately, at an inaugural meeting of HIM in Waldport, Oregon, on 14 September 1975 Bo and Peep had promised that their deaths, resurrection and translation by UFO would occur within six months. When no assassin obliged with the necessary act, they hastily revised their

THE 'ALIENS' KNEW THEY WOULD BE ASSASSINATED AND LEFT FOR DEAD IN THE STREET.

Below: ***Unholy alliance – a 17th-century representation of witches, imps and Satan. Some ufologists would now add UFOs and aliens to the forms that evil may take.***

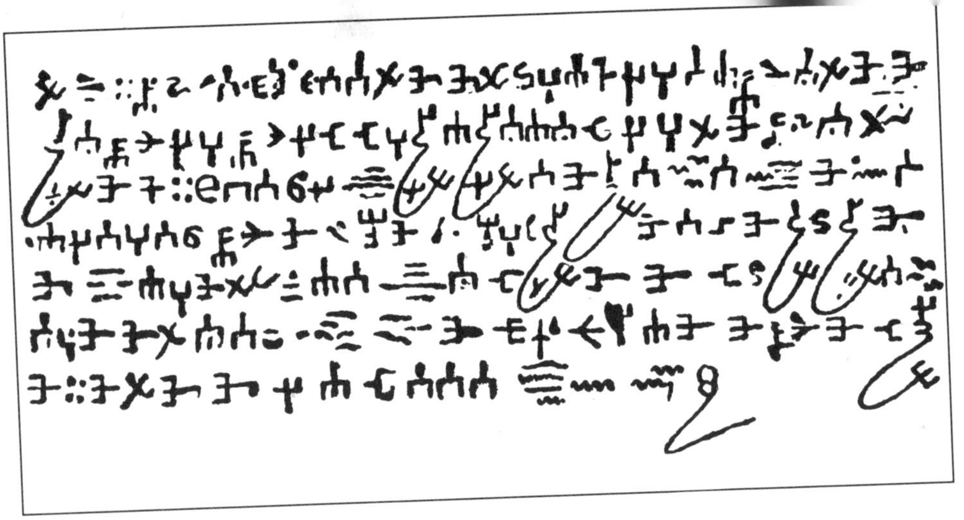

Above: *John Ashton's intriguing volume* **The Devil In Britain And America,** *published in 1896, contains this curious script, which purports to be 'the only known specimen of the Devil's handwriting'.*

Above: *The Devil gains a small victory – and succeeds in stealing the church at Over, Cheshire, as told in a local legend.*

Below right: *French Dr Jacques Vallée, who maintains that the UFO phenomenon is a 'control system' that 'acts on humans and uses humans' – although he does not suggest that the controlling power is either divine or demonic.*

timetable and announced they would remain on Earth for at least a further ten years. The number of devotees soon declined drastically and, 15 years later, Bo and Peep were still on Earth, living a nomadic existence with their few remaining followers in Wyoming and Texas.

A similar fate befell the cult that grew up around the British Columbian channeller Robin McPherson (a.k.a. Estelle), whose extra-terrestrial contact Ox-Ho predicted that prodigious natural disasters would begin on Earth on 22 November 1969. The 'Chosen' – i.e. members of the cult, Light Affiliates – would be removed beforehand by the Space Brothers and returned when the Earth had recovered. No major disaster of any kind began on Earth that day.

It remains to be seen whether the prediction of Ruth E. Norman, channeller for an entity called URIEL (Universal Radiant Infinite Eternal Light) will come true. According to URIEL, spacecraft from the 33 members of the Interplanetary Confederation will land in the year 2001, to usher in a 1000-year epoch of peace, contentment and cultural achievement.

TIME IS RUNNING OUT FAST...WAVES OF SENSELESS IRRATIONAL VIOLENCE WILL DROWN THE EARTH.

SUBVERSIVE INVASIONS

The cosmologies of the various UFO cults are wildly different – far more incompatible with each other than any established Earthly religion. The California-based One World Family, for instance, declare that they will one day take over the government of the USA and the administration of the United Nations – but not before all professing Christians have been 'eliminated'. In contrast, the Aetherians have no political ambitions, and maintain that the Christian prophet is recognized as an intergalactic 'Master' who lives on, or near, Venus – which happens also to be the alleged abode of Ashtar, the One World Family's extra-terrestrial contact. Allen-Michael Noonan, the leader of the sect, claims to be the sole authentic mouthpiece for Ashtar – but Tuella, of the Utah-based cult, Ashtar Space Command, regularly channels messages of a gentler nature from an 'interplanetary space commander' of the same name.

All these cults differ fundamentally, however, with the small band of commentators who see UFOs not as harbingers of peace and plenty, but as unambiguously evil. Chief among these is probably linguist and former diplomat Gordon Creighton, editor of the international UFO journal *Flying Saucer Review*. Creighton's own theory is that *djinns*, supernatural creatures who work on behalf of the forces of evil and can take on human form, are UFOs in appropriate cultural disguise. Curiously, Creighton has an apocalyptic view of the present era that is not far removed from the beliefs of some 'space brother'-types of UFO cult who are expecting the End Times to begin at any moment:

'Time is running out fast. All the indications are that before the close of this century, cataclysmic and apocalyptic events will rend the planet. As the waves of senseless, irrational violence rise higher and higher on the Earth...who can doubt that certain of the "UFO entities" have a hand in the wrecking, and in the stirring of the nauseating brew?'

How he knows these things, Creighton does not reveal. But there is a long fundamentalist Christian tradition of identifying UFOs with the work of the Devil. As early as 1954 Gordon Cove offered the novel insight that 'Satan is the cleverest military genius ever known.' Exactly which battles in history he has planned and won, Cove did not say, but was certain that the aliens aboard UFOs were possessed by the Devil, even when appearing to be most benign.

Commentator Dan Lloyd likewise sees the UFO cults who look forward to mass contact with our intergalactic guardians as deluded: their 'distorted religious longings' are directed toward entities who merely appear benign in order to win our trust and thereby subvert humanity. He follows ufologist Jacques Vallée's suggestion in his book *Messengers of Deception* that the UFO phenomenon is 'a control system which acts on humans and uses humans.'

Vallée points to recurrent patterns in UFO cases that echo patterns of behaviour by evil spirits, goblins and other creatures from folklore, and suggests that something – perhaps human, and perhaps not – is making such patterns. Lloyd first argues that UFOs are not from another physical dimension, but are 'deliberately distorted etheric effects, and it should surprise no one to learn that such effects can influence physical matter and create, in turn, physical effects' and then identifies the maker of the patterns noted by Vallée: 'Behind whatever human group may be active in this area, there hovers the invisible presence of...the cosmic being who has been known since ancient Persian times as Ahriman. In the Bible he is known as Satan.'

EXTRA-TERRESTRIAL SALVATION

From this brief survey of the various points of contact between UFOs and religious beliefs, a number of things emerge. We previously suggested that such beliefs rest on a confusion between the *scientific* concept of other planes of being, distinct from but equal to our own, and the *religious* apprehension of a quite different kind of 'other dimension', the absolute reality that informs all existence.

This confusion is nowhere more evident than in the message of The Two, who seemed to think that Heaven, or something like it, could be reached in a spaceship. Such a literal, physical religious cosmology has not been contemplated by any major religion since the Middle Ages.

In conventional religious terms, there is no conflict between the levels of reality inhabited by God and those of parallel universes or additional dimensions. The Creator of one universe is still the Creator of all the others; and the God that created humanity also created ufonauts. But what, in effect, many of the cultists have done is to create a kind of substitute set of gods – the aliens, 'space brothers' and the rest,

Above: ***Scale model of a UFO constructed by the Aetherius Society. Note the resemblance to the UFO that George Adamski claimed to have seen in California in the early 1950s.***

Above: *A UFO, caught on film by Guy B. Marquand, skims the hills near Riverside, California.*

who will come down like cosmic cavalry to save humanity from itself.

Leaving aside the question of how many of the major world religions would regard this belief as heresy, the UFO cults actually have little in common besides a common faith in some kind of extra-terrestrial salvation. If *all* these cults have any claim to truth, the immediate regions of space around Earth must be unusually crowded with our intergalactic brethren.

If these cults *are* in touch with genuine UFO entities, there are only a few logical conclusions to draw. One is that the ufonauts themselves are confused, with no greater claim to the truth than anyone on Earth. Or they themselves are at the mercy of rival systems of thought, and for all we know may be deeply hostile to one another's beliefs. Or they may simply be hopeless at prophecy, which also puts them on much the same level as anyone on Earth. Or, worst of all, they are cosmic cats, playing with the dying mouse of humanity.

This leads us to one further possible explanation. We have seen in previous chapters how both UFOs and their occupants, in all kinds of context, indulge in apparently meaningless, often contradictory, and most often simply incomprehensible behaviour: disguise, trickery, deceit, cruelty that, if the reports are to be believed, does not balk at rape or murder. One does not have to believe that UFOs are evil to wonder if the 'messages to mankind' and the cults they inspire are not simply another facet of this taunting game. If, that is, it is a game.

THE UFOs ARE COSMIC CATS PLAYING A TAUNTING GAME WITH THE DYING MOUSE OF HUMANITY.

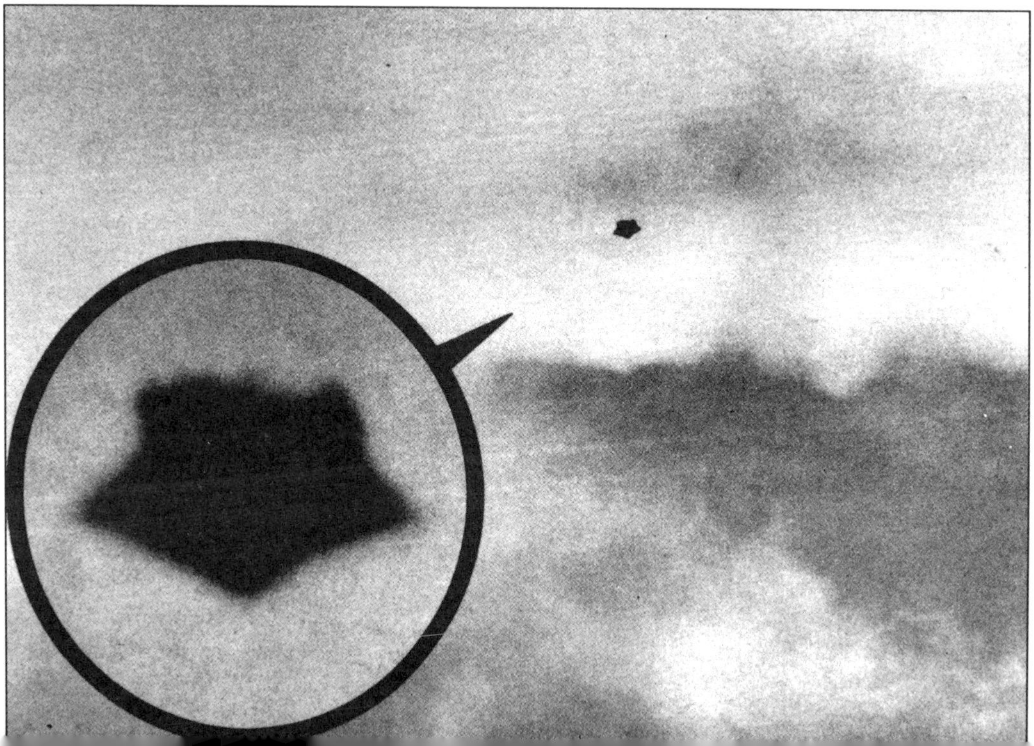

Right: *A black UFO photographed as, allegedly, it hovered for almost half an hour over Shiogama City, north of Tokyo, Japan, on 27 September 1986. If the picture is genuine, the shape of the craft is not unlike the all-black F-117A 'Stealth' strike aircraft – but that cannot hover.*

FATAL ATTRACTION

Most attempts to explain the UFO phenomenon assume that there is some coherent purpose behind their presence here – and even a game, even the one a cat plays with a mouse, has a purpose. The struggle of most serious ufologists has been to discover that purpose; the UFO cultists believe they have the answer. But such an assumption may be the most naïve error that ufology has ever made, the fatal result of supposing in the first place that aliens are in any way at all like us.

In his book *Perspectives: a Radical Examination of the Alien Abduction Phenomenon*, ufologist John Spencer presents his 'Moth Proposal', which is possibly the most successful attempt yet made to reconcile all the contradictions within the reams of evidence for UFOs.

Spencer notes first that if certain sense-receptor cells in the brains of both humans and other mammals are not stimulated very early in an animal's life, they do not develop. This means that if, say, a child's long-sightedness goes undetected for very long, the brain is incapable of interpreting objects at close range properly, even when the image reaching the retina and hence the brain has been corrected with glasses. The brain simply has not developed a mechanism for dealing with this kind of input.

Spencer suggests that UFOs have had the same effect on people today (and one might add, throughout recorded history). We do not see UFOs correctly – hence the plethora of shapes and sizes reported – because we have not been conditioned to see whatever it is they really are. And he quotes the Russian UFO researcher Vladimir Rubstov, saying that an image is created in the mind 'as a result of the interaction between the sensory data and "anticipating patterns" that are kept deep in human memory. Seeing a completely new object means building promptly a new pattern to assimilate the non-standard sensory information. Such a pattern is usually constructed by association.' Rubstov remarks that this is no guarantee that the mental image will conform with 'the real structure of the observed phenomenon, and [this] may lead to various illusions'.

Spencer then describes the view of the world enjoyed by a family of moths living near a major motorway. What, he asks, would the moths understand of human society from their observations of vehicles, the occasional person walking from a car to the emergency telephone, or even relieving himself behind a bush? Would moths assume that 'the "visitations" of our vehicles are for a specific purpose relating to moths? From their interaction with telegraph poles, could they ever understand the telephone? Would they assume that the lighting, switched on when they are most active, is a device for luring and killing them? From their perspective, could they ever understand the true meaning of the lights, could they comprehend that when we constructed them, we never even thought of moths?'

Our mistake, Spencer suggests, in trying to understand UFOs, is the assumption that we are the object of the aliens' interest, rather than, like the moth dashing itself against a street light, 'caught up in something that may not even concern us'.

Any attempt to answer the crucial questions that John Spencer has raised must address once again the vexed question of where UFOs may come from.

Above: ***Contactee Paul Villa claimed to have snapped this UFO near Volcano Mountain, outside Albuquerque, New Mexico, in April 1965. All the many UFO pictures taken by Villa have been shown to be fakes.***

HUMANITY WILL BE DESTROYED IN SOMETHING THAT MAY NOT EVEN CONCERN IT.

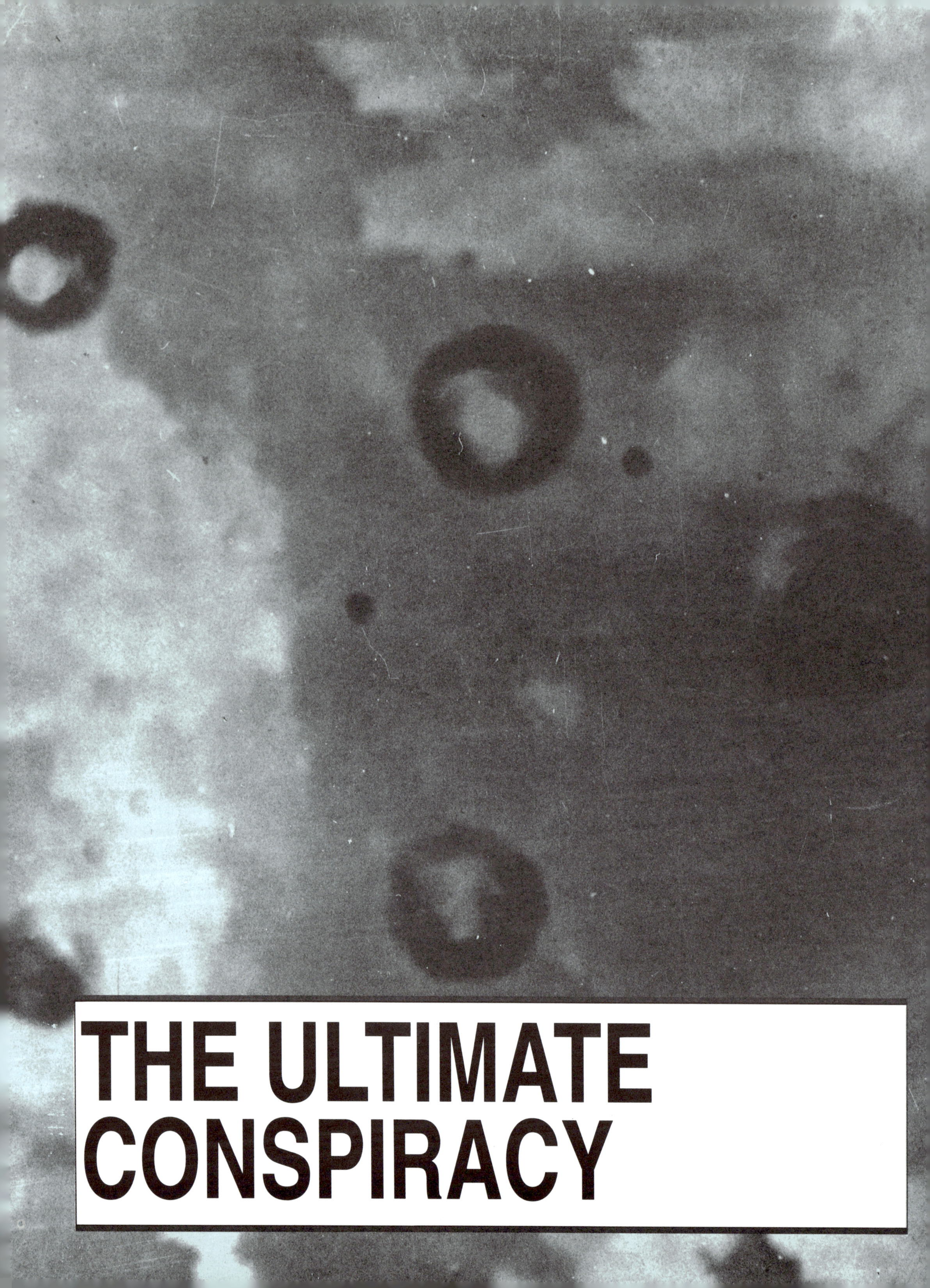

THE ULTIMATE CONSPIRACY

The 'thorough' scientific study, funded by the USAF, was designed to end the speculation about UFOs for once and for all. When its cover was blown, the public demanded to know exactly what the Pentagon was hiding.

If UFOs do not come from other inhabited planets in our galaxy, or from even further afield, how can we account for the widespread belief that they do?

When Kenneth Arnold opened the modern UFO era in 1947 with his sighting over the Cascade Mountains, it was perhaps inevitable, in the atmosphere of post-war America, that people would jump to the conclusion that he had seen craft from another world. The possibility that space might be explored, possibly even settled, had been glimpsed in the development of rocket technology in the USA before World War 2. During the war that technology advanced spectacularly in Germany, but these projects were always ambiguous, for while space was the 'last frontier' for humanity to conquer, there was also a more cynical use to which the technology could be put. And that was to provide vehicles with which to deliver weapons of mass destruction. For this was also the dawn of the nuclear age, with its 'balance of terror' and strategy of mutually assured destruction, or 'MAD'.

In 1947, Americans were deeply concerned that the USSR would soon develop nuclear weapons of its own – which would, in theory, make an invasion of the USA feasible. Kenneth Arnold's sighting of 'flying saucers' came at a time when the Western world, and the USA in particular, was obsessed with a fear of Communist invasion. Besides the military threat, there were fifth columnists, agitators, sympathizers and spies – 'the enemy within' – to beware of.

Worse, the Reds were prepared to invade

Opposite: ***Published in the*** **Irish Teen-Age Times** ***in March 1950, this obviously faked still was hailed as the first-ever photograph of a flying saucer. It was accompanied by the sensational revelation that flying saucers were space stations loaded with nuclear bombs, capable of being positioned anywhere above the Earth. The story did not divulge who controlled the craft. This was not the first time that UFOs were to be identified as secret weapons.***

Below: ***A UFO leaves a trail of vapour or smoke as it streaks across the sky at Madre de Dios, Peru, in 1952. Was this a secret terrestrial weapon being tested, or an alien craft in yet another unexpected guise?***

your mind. Since the 1930s it had been suspected that the Communist authorities used far-reaching psychological techniques to remould the opinions of dissidents. Veterans of the Korean war 'confirmed' this nightmare, with accounts of the most soul-destroying and violent attempts to 'brainwash' Western prisoners of war.

In 1947, then, the intriguing notion of life in space combined with political anxieties about invasions of all kinds, to produce a 'logical' conclusion about Arnold's sighting: if these silvery disks were not from an Earthly power, they had to be invaders from outer space. The reaction to Arnold's sighting was simply a very early sign of the conditions that produced the long nuclear winter of the Cold War. The fretful temper of the times was reflected in films of the era, which portrayed aliens in flying saucers as ready to colonize the world and, given the slightest opportunity, to enslave humanity in the process.

The extra-terrestrial hypothesis (ETH) has remained popular ever since partly because the media have tended to ignore alternative interpretations of UFO events – and partly because similar kinds of fears and uncertainties to those common in 1947 have remained with us ever since.

But there may be a more sinister reason why the ETH has remained the paramount interpretation of UFOs.

Above: ***Falling on stony ground – Connie Menger, wife of contactee Howard Menger, talks to arch-sceptic Dr Edward U. Condon, whose study of UFO phenomena effectively ended official US Air Force interest in the subject.***

THE TRUTH BEHIND THE 'INVADERS FROM OUTER SPACE' WAS EVEN MORE SINISTER.

DEBUNKING EXERCISE

Many serious UFO researchers hoped that when the University of Colorado began a thorough scientific study of the UFO phenomenon in 1966, government and military sources would have little choice but to open all their files on the subject to the research team and, perhaps, to public gaze as well. In charge of the project was a distinguished physicist, Dr Edward Condon, and the funding – all $572,146 of it – came courtesy of the USAF, which had finally agreed to the study under pressure from Congress. Condon's committee started work on 6 October 1966. Its brief was to sift the USAF's mountain of UFO sighting reports – an archive that contained nearly 20 years' worth of material – and draw whatever conclusions it could.

As far as both public and ufologists were concerned, the mystery that had baffled everyone for almost two decades would be given the kind of attention it deserved. That hope must surely have been swept away for all time in the autumn of

Right: ***Robert J. Low, who set up Condon's study at the University of Colorado so that it would show 'there is no reality' to UFO sightings.***

1968, when Dr David Saunders, a scientist at Colorado, blew the cover on what was supposed to be the most elaborate and exhaustive study of UFOs ever undertaken.

Out of disgust at the way the work was actually being done, Saunders published a memo that the committee's co-ordinator, Robert Low, had written in August 1966 while negotiating the contract for the work at Colorado. From it, one can only infer that the university was looking for ways to meet a presumably unofficial – even secret – Air Force brief to make the study a debunking exercise instead of a cool appraisal of the evidence.

Low wrote: 'Our study would be conducted almost exclusively by non-believers who...could and probably would add an impressive body of evidence that there is no reality to the observations. The trick would be, I think, to describe the project so that, to the public, it would appear a totally objective study but, to the scientific community, would present a group of non-believers trying their best to be objective but having an almost zero expectation of finding a saucer.'

Saunders further charged Low and Condon with ignoring the most difficult evidence in favour of weak cases that would bolster the impression that the UFO enigma was a chimera.

The Condon Report, as *The Scientific Study of UFOs* is usually known, was published on 9 January 1969. It was a 1485-page dossier, and in deference to busy journalists Condon's summary of the report was printed first – and the summary was all that the media initially reported. The key finding was: 'Careful consideration of the record...leads us to conclude that further extensive study of UFOs probably cannot be justified in the expectation that science will be advanced thereby.'

'KOOKS'

For those who bothered to read the rest of the report, Condon's summary was bizarre, for it bore no relation to what his committee had actually written. Of the 87 UFO sightings that it had documented and investigated, about 25 per cent were admitted to be inexplicable. In a further 8 per cent, the debunkers had become desperate indeed as they strove to find 'natural' explanations for the otherwise inconceivable.

One analysis concludes implausibly: 'This unusual sighting should therefore be assigned to the category of some almost certainly natural phenomenon which is so rare that it apparently has never been reported before or since.' Any real scientist would have sought at once for other, similar

Above: ***Serious UFO studies have always been hampered by hoaxes and fake photographs. This shot was taken in July 1952 by Gianpetro Monguzzi. Ostensibly of an entity standing beside a landed UFO in the Bernina Mountains of Italy, it was later admitted to be a hoax made by using tabletop models and photomontage.***

UFOLOGISTS WERE FURIOUS AT THE GOVERNMENT'S ATTEMPTS TO HOODWINK THEM.

deliberately? Was he a willing dupe of the USAF and the US government, 'just following orders'? Or was he chosen for his role by those who knew his scepticism, and knew that his conclusions would serve their own mysterious purposes? Edward Condon was certainly a lifelong debunker of UFOs, who delighted in regaling people with tales of the crankier devotees of UFO lore and who regarded even serious ufologists simply as 'kooks'.

But the US government itself has always taken UFOs seriously. The USAF set up its first UFO unit, Project Sign, on 22 January 1948. Its task was to try to assess whether the recent, persistent and growing evidence of mysterious and hitherto unknown aerial craft in the skies signalled a technological breakthrough by a potential enemy (in short, the USSR).

Above: ***Traces allegedly left by a UFO when it landed at Morrill Farm, Piermont, New Hampshire, during the winter of 1974.***

Right: ***The USAF Project Blue Book's last commanding officer, Major H. Quintanilla, with his staff. This tiny team was expected to investigate and evaluate thousands of UFO reports every year.***

reports – but there is evidence that Condon did not allow his committee to address themselves seriously to the whole 25,000 or so reports held by the USAF's UFO-watching unit, Project Blue Book. Ufologists have held ever since that the Condon Report is one of the grossest examples of government trying to hoodwink the people on a matter of major importance.

Was Condon, in fact, covering up

A COVER-UP

There was every reason to believe such a hypothesis. It is now known – and was surely known to the security agencies of the time – that among the papers found at the secret V-2 rocket proving grounds at Peenemunde in Germany were plans for a saucer-shaped flying machine. During the same period Avro Canada were developing for the US Navy the VZ-9AV, a saucer-shaped craft intended to fly at 300 knots at

30,000 ft. No one knew that this revolutionary design's best performance was in fact to be a rather sedate 30 knots at a maximum altitude of 3 ft. The point was that saucer-like flying vehicles were believed to be viable and potentially very powerful.

By early 1949 those working on Project Sign had enough data to conclude that while UFOs might pose no security threat, their technical capacities were so extraordinary that they could only be extraterrestrial. The Air Force's reaction was surprisingly violent, and swift: Chief of Staff General Hoyt Vandenberg ordered all copies of the report to be burned, and then the USAF shut the project down. A new team, disconcertingly code-named Project Grudge, was set up on 11 February 1949 to make a fresh assessment. Grudge proposed a campaign of debunking.

In the light of the reaction to Sign's report and Grudge's advice, it seems strange that three years later, in March 1952, the USAF set up Project Blue Book to collect sighting reports and investigate them. But Blue Book's budget and staff were totally inadequate to the size of its task. Many commentators have wondered if this inadequacy was deliberate, and if the project's real purpose was simply to act as a front to reassure an anxious public that the origins of UFOs lay either in misidentifications of natural phenomena or aircraft, or in occasional hoaxes.

Blue Book's astronomy consultant, Dr J. Allen Hynek, wrote years later:

'Blue Book was a cover-up to the extent that the assigned problem was glossed over for one reason or another...[in the 18 years of the project's existence] I do not recall even one serious discussion of methodology, of improving the process of data gathering or of techniques of comprehensive interrogation...The charge was frequently made that the publicly visible air force "investigation" of UFOs was merely a front for a real investigation being carried on somewhere "higher up"...for instance, one time when I inquired into the specifics of a certain case, I was told by the Pentagon's chief scientist that he had been

Top left: ***Roscoe H. Hillenkoetter, pictured in the rank of captain USN. It has been claimed that later, as an admiral and first head of the CIA, he was involved in an 'above top secret' panel charged with handling contacts with alien civilizations.***

Above: ***A German V-2 rocket launching pad. Trials of these rockets after World War 2 in the USA almost certainly gave rise to erroneous UFO reports. This gave the military the opportunity to use 'UFOs' as a cover for many other secret activities, and sometimes for its own blunders.***

Right: ***This UFO was photographed at Lake Tiorati, New York on 18 December 1966.***

BEHIND THE SMOKESCREEN, TECHNOLOGY, DRUGS AND PSYCHOLOGICAL MANIPULATION COULD BE ILLICITLY TESTED ON INNOCENT VICTIMS.

advised by those at a much higher level to tell me "not to pursue the matter further".'

What did the Pentagon have to hide?

DRUGS

William H. Spaulding, of the Arizona-based organization Ground Saucer Watch (GSW), has developed the 'Federal Hypothesis', the result of a careful analysis of hundreds of top secret UFO-related documents declassified under the Freedom of Information Act. The Federal Hypothesis offers a new solution to the puzzle of what governments are not telling us about UFOs.

Spaulding noted that areas of apparently high UFO activity in the USA were also near proving grounds for secret weapons and aircraft. (The same, as it happens, is also true in the UK.) He also realized that waves of American UFO sightings frequently followed moments of crisis for the US government, and cited the 'flap' in New Mexico and West Texas that followed the Soviets' successful launch of Sputnik II (only 30 days after Sputnik I) in November 1957 as an especially shocking example. At the time, the US space programme was suffering repeated, ignominious and nationally televised failures of its own satellite rocket launchers.

Spaulding suspected that many other aspects of the UFO phenomenon might be attributable to interference run by the CIA, and perhaps by a rogue cell within the organization. Close encounters and abductions may be the result of illicitly administering mind-expanding drugs to the unwary (the CIA did do this, under controlled conditions, in the 1960s). If that is so, the agency gathers much useful information. Not only are the victims' reactions monitored, but so too are media and general public reaction to accounts of events that are real in the mind of the witness but incredible to almost anyone else.

MEN IN BLACK

This may be the explanation for some abductee cases. It may also explain one of the weirder and more frightening 'side-effects' of some UFO sightings, the visits that some witnesses receive from the 'men in black' or MIB.

A typical instance occurred in Canada in 1981. At around 9.30 pm on the evening of 2 October, 16-year-old Grant Breiland saw a UFO from his home in Victoria, British Columbia, in Canada. It resembled an inverted dome, bright white in colour, with a red light that moved around the dome in a regular pattern. Above, below and on each side of the object were further white lights.

These details he saw by looking through binoculars and through the powerful zoom lens of his Ricoh SLR camera. Breiland used his CB radio to discover if anyone was on nearby Mount Tolmie, three miles distant, who could also see the object. A young man of 19, identified by the case investigators only as 'N.B.', 'came back' on the CB and confirmed that he too could see the object. After moving around the sky for about half an hour, the UFO vanished, like a light being turned out.

The next day, the two young men met for the first time to discuss their sighting. Breiland had never seen a UFO before and had read only one book on the subject when he was aged about 12. He could not remember its title.

The next Monday, at about 3.30 pm, Breiland was in a local supermarket when he saw two sun-tanned men watching him. They were dressed in extremely dark blue suits, shirts and shoes. Neither had eyelashes, and their eyes reflected no light. They approached him, and one asked, in a monotonous, mechanical voice: 'What is your name?' Breiland refused to tell him. The other then asked him where he lived. When Breiland again refused to help, they turned and walked away stiffly in complete unison. Breiland followed them as far as the edge of a muddy building plot, which they began to cross. Distracted momentarily, he looked away; when he turned back, they had vanished. He followed their path across the plot, but was so alarmed when he realized that they had left no footprints that he fled the scene.

MIB typically resemble G-men from a 1940s or 1950s Hollywood B-movie, and they may actually produce some form of ID and claim to be from a government department or, occasionally, a UFO research group. And they almost always know of witnesses' experiences even before they have reported them to anyone, and threaten that the witnesses or a member of their family will suffer if they reveal anything

Below: ***A UFO over Bulawayo? Photographer Barney Wayne was uncertain about what the curious object could be. The most likely candidate is a lenticular cloud – if, indeed, the object is in the sky and not solely on the film.***

Right: ***Sketch by Connecticut ufologist Albert Bender of a 'man in black' (MIB) who visited him in September 1953. The MIB so terrified Bender that he abandoned UFO research and did not tell the story of his encounter for several years. Despite the sometimes horrific threats that MIB utter, they have never been known to follow them up when a witness breaks silence. For this and other reasons, some researchers believe MIB are apparitions, while others suggest they may be real enough, but part of a long-term clandestine experiment in the psychology of fear.***

about it. Another weird aspect of the MIB is their transport. The cars they drive are usually Cadillacs or some other luxury model – which looks brand-new but has been out of production for years.

One of the strangest MIB encounters occurred to Dr Herbert Hopkins, who investigated the abduction of David Stephens in Maine in 1975, and his son. In September 1976, not only was Dr Hopkins visited by a MIB, who apart from being dressed 'like an undertaker' was deadly pale, totally bald – lacking even eyebrows or eyelashes – but was apparently wearing lipstick; but, a few days later, his son John received a visit from a man and a woman who, if not a stereotype MIB pair, were certainly quite peculiar.

They visited John Hopkins and his wife Maureen at home, and asked them a number of personal questions. While this was going on, the man kept 'pawing and fondling' the woman in a startling, intimate manner, and from time to time asked John if he was doing it correctly! When John left the room, the man asked Maureen 'how she was made', and if she had any photographs of herself naked. They left without even saying goodbye.

In this case, the MIB involved made no threats, but the threats they do make are never fulfilled: it is as if they are actually testing the effectiveness of empty menaces.

SECRET OPERATIONS

The creation of a series of such unlikely events – enough to fuel the mystery and the media, and keep ufologists busy – would serve two purposes. Bear in mind that the 'cover-up' has largely succeeded in diverting the scientific community from the UFO phenomenon already, by exercises like the Condon Report and persistent official denials (now, perhaps, seen to be true, in an unexpected way!) of the 'reality' of UFOs. First, the events that witnesses describe are so outlandish that most ordinary people tend to dismiss them as incredible, while the media make fun of them – and consequently no scientific body will investigate closely. And so, behind this smokescreen, secret technology, unusual aircraft designs and psychological manipulations can freely be tested.

For example, since the late 1980s there have been many reports from Puerto Rico that feature aircraft, notably the US Navy's F-14 Tomcats, chasing UFOs. Here are summaries of three of those reports.

At around 8.30 pm on 4 July 1989, F-14s from Roosevelt Roads Naval Air Station at Ceiba were seen by witnesses from the nearby town of Luquillo, in pursuit of 'a very big and brilliant blue-white star' that performed bizarre manoeuvres near Mount El Yunque before heading south-east across the Sierra de Luquillo, with the jets still trailing it.

In the evening of 22 June 1990, three witnesses saw four F-14s chasing 'a round ball of yellow light with a very bright red light in its center' that was flying in a south-westerly direction over the Rio Guyate near Route 52, in the eastern part of the island. The F-14s were followed in turn by an AWACS radar surveillance aircraft.

At 5.30 pm on 19 December 1990, residents of Caguas, also in eastern Puerto Rico, saw unmarked military helicopters apparently in pursuit of a similar yellow and red light 'as big as a 747 [jumbo jet]' and 'flying totally noiselessly', which disappeared among the mountains.

The US Navy's Atlantic Fleet Weapons Training Facility (AFWTF) has its headquarters hard by Roosevelt Roads NAS, and controls two huge ocean firing ranges – Alfa, some 120,000 square miles in area, to the north and east of the island,

and Bravo, 74,000 square miles in extent, to the south-east. Among the hardware tested by AFWTF are cruise missiles and electronic warfare devices. The US Navy is also funding development of advanced fighters using unconventional airfoils – swept-forward wings, for instance. Any of these could either be deliberately disguised as a UFO to cover tests that the local population might otherwise find objectionable (such as flying a cruise missile over populated areas) or could easily be mistaken for a 'flying saucer' – especially when flying at dusk, and especially if of unconventional shape.

Two instances cited by Spaulding will further illustrate how the UFO phenomenon is used as a cover for secret operations.

In October and November 1975, the North American Air Defense Command (NORAD) received a series of UFO reports from USAF bases and missile sites in northern Montana, northern North Dakota, northern Minnesota, Maine and Michigan. Common factors were that few of the sightings showed on radar; stationary lights; and lights that flashed on and off in various colours.

In one instance on 8 November, two F-106 fighters armed with missiles were scrambled from Great Falls, Montana, to

In 1990 a number of UFO sightings in Puerto Rico involved US Navy F-14 Tomcats (top) *and USAF AWACS* (above), *apparently in hot pursuit of seemingly alien craft. However, Puerto Rico is home to the headquarters of two vast US Navy ocean firing ranges, where cruise missiles* (left) *and other still more exotic hardware are routinely tested. It would serve the military's public relations only too well if the public were to ascribe highly secret craft or test firings that went awry to 'UFOs'.*

investigate seven objects flying at between 10,000 and 13,000 ft that the 24th NORAD Region had picked up on radar, and that could be seen as lights from the ground. The fighter pilots were instructed to fly no lower than 12,000 ft and at moderate speed (the F-106 is capable of Mach 2, or about 1500 mph). When the jets approached, the lights went out. The fighters returned to base without having made contact with the 'unknowns'.

Spaulding concluded that this was not a classic case of 'saucers spying on military bases'. The 'entire November flap,' he wrote, 'represents a contrived military exercise, possibly involving both US and Canadian Special Forces, to covertly test detection capability and response...The UFOs were stealth (low detectability) helicopters...The whole "crisis"...reeks of a military mission [in which] a few individuals [know] the facts and the operators within the military system are kept in the dark.'

Stealth technology – seen in the USAF's B-2 bomber, F117A fighter (sometimes, before its public unveiling, erroneously identified as the F-19) and the experimental A12-ATA attack aircraft – has been under development since 1966. In 1975 a USAF mobile radar unit picked up an aircraft leaving Edwards AFB, California, at over 460 mph. In one sweep of the radar, the 'blip' had vanished – a feat possible, in theory, only if the target had accelerated to over 2000 mph.

Above: ***The USAF's B-2 'Stealth' bomber, which is virtually invisible to radar, thanks to a combination of shape, materials and a powerful armoury of electronic counter-measures carried on board. The aircraft and the effects of its technology were so unorthodox that both were more than once linked to UFOs during their development phase.***

IN THE UPROAR NO ONE NOTICED THAT THE AFFAIR CLEARLY INDICATED THE ORIGIN OF THE CRASHED SAUCERS.

Right: ***TV producer Jaime Shandera, who in 1984 received a package of allegedly top-secret documents that, if genuine, had world-shaking implications.***

In other words, this was another case of a UFO spying on a military installation, and was reported as such. And in fact, in a sense, it was exactly that – a plane testing the effectiveness of stealth technology against a military unit that had deliberately been given no warning of its presence. The aircraft switched on its electronic counter-measures systems in that sweep of the radar, and became electronically 'invisible'. How many civilian air traffic controllers reporting UFOs on their radar screens have been the unwitting victims of such tests?

CONSPIRACY

The difficulty with the Federal Hypothesis is that, like all the other UFO conspiracy theories, it cannot be conclusively proven. But it does fit many of the known facts better than most other conspiracy theories, and certainly better than the extra-terrestrial hypothesis. Nowhere is this better illustrated than in the case of the 'documentary proof' and 'highly placed intelligence sources' cited by those who

have been promoting the 'Majestic 12' legend since the early 1980s.

Los Angeles TV producer Jaime Shandera received a package in his mail on 11 December 1984 that, if it was genuine, was of world-shaking importance. Inside were photocopies of two documents, one dated 24 September 1947, the other 18 November 1952. The first was signed by US President Harry S Truman. The second was addressed to President Dwight D. Eisenhower by Admiral Roscoe H. Hillenkoetter. Both were marked TOP SECRET.

The first was perhaps the more momentous of the two. It purported to be a classified executive order from Truman to Secretary of Defense James Forrestal, and it authorized him, after due consultation with nuclear scientist Dr Vannevar Bush, to establish a board of suitably qualified persons to be answerable directly and only to the president, and to be known as 'Majestic 12' (or 'Majic-12' or simply 'MJ-12'). Their job was to investigate the case of the flying saucer that had crashed near Roswell, N.M., in July 1947.

Here, it seemed, was proof that the crash, long a subject of rumour and speculation among ufologists of all persuasions, had really happened. The second document backed the first. It was a top secret briefing for the newly elected president on the members and progress of the MJ-12 group. It consisted of 12 eminent scientists, engineers, military men and intelligence experts – some of whom, such as Hillenkoetter, combined more than one of these roles – and even included Harvard astronomer Dr Donald Menzel, who in his public utterances was a ferocious opponent of any suggestion that UFOs were remotely 'real'.

Menzel's presence seemed at first sight like a classic case of the sheep in wolf's clothing. To scholars of UFO conspiracy theories, Hillenkoetter's involvement was still more fascinating. The Admiral had not been purely a Navy man. He was also the first Director of the CIA (also established in September 1947; Hillenkoetter had also headed its predecessor, the Central Intelligence Group, since 1 May that year). He retired from the Navy in June 1957 and soon afterwards joined the Board of Governors of the National Investigations Committee on Aerial Phenomena, one of the first and most influential civilian UFO organizations. Conspiracy theorists have always maintained that Hillenkoetter – once a spy, always a spy – was a fifth columnist of the first water. Here, it seemed, was conclusive proof.

In view of the somewhat cataclysmic nature of the MJ-12 documents it seems strange that it was more than three years (on 29 May 1987) before Shandera, along with his associates, the writers W.L. Moore and Charles Berlitz, and crashed-saucer

Above: ***Dwight D. Eisenhower in 1944. There is circumstantial evidence that when US President he inspected evidence of alien contact held at Wright-Patterson AFB.***

Below: ***Dr Donald H. Menzel, renowned for his debunking of UFO reports.***

Right: ***Stanton Friedman, the nuclear physicist who has amassed much evidence that shows, to his satisfaction at least, that the US government has a secret collection of crashed UFOs and dead aliens.***

expert Stanton T. Friedman, made them public. The quartet claimed to have contacted a 'highly placed military intelligence operative' who could authenticate the story.

However, the 'highly placed' intelligence source turned out to be a lowly USAF sergeant once found guilty of falsifying official documents, and the papers themselves soon took a battering. Meticulous research by ufologist Philip J. Klass revealed that the machine used to type the Truman 'executive order' of 1947 was a Smith-Corona model that had not been manufactured until 1963. Hillenkoetter had dated his memorandum to Eisenhower in an odd hybrid of civilian and military styles and signed himself 'Roscoe H. Hillenkoetter'. Neither of these forms appear before or since in any of his voluminous surviving correspondence.

Finally, Klass's close inspection of the signature on the Truman document showed beyond reasonable doubt that it was a photocopy of the signature on a letter from Truman to Vannevar Bush, written on 1 October 1947. And as the Hillenkoetter memo of 1952 refers specifically to the Truman 'special classified executive order' of 1947, it follows that both are fakes.

There is indeed a UFO conspiracy, but exactly who is conspiring against whom is far from obvious. And what no one seems to have noticed in the uproar over the MJ-12 affair is the clear indication that the 'crashed saucer' stories are not only hoaxes, but would appear to have their origins inside US intelligence. Some part of the US intelligence network is still interested in fuelling one of the most outlandish aspects of the UFO enigma. The Majestic 12 affair may not prove the Federal Hypothesis, but it certainly helps to make it more credible than any other conspiracy theory concerning UFOs.

Below: ***Philip Klass, relentless UFO sceptic and tireless researcher, stands beside a display board showing material from the Gulf Breeze case, one of the most controversial modern claims for a sustained series of encounters with a UFO.***